Fortnite For Teens

The Complete 3-Book Bundle

Your Ultimate Guides for

Winning Fortnite Battle Royale

EVERYT

BY

Ultimate Game Guides

Fortnite: Battle Royale

© Copyright 2018 by Ultimate Game Guides

The following eBook is reproduced below with the
goal of providing information that is as accurate
and reliable as possible. Regardless, purchasing
this eBook can be seen as consent to the fact that
both the publisher and the author of this book are
in no way experts on the topics discussed within
and that any recommendations or suggestions that
are made herein are for entertainment purposes
only. Professionals should be consulted as needed
prior to undertaking any of the action endorsed
herein.

This declaration is deemed fair and valid by both
the American Bar Association and the Committee
of Publishers Association and is legally binding
throughout the United States.

Furthermore, the transmission, duplication or
reproduction of any of the following work
including specific information will be considered
an illegal act irrespective of if it is done

electronically or in print. This extends to creating a secondary or tertiary copy of the work or a recorded copy and is only allowed with an expressed written consent from the Publisher. All additional right reserved.

The information in the following pages is broadly considered to be a truthful and accurate account of facts, and as such any inattention, use or misuse of the information in question by the reader will render any resulting actions solely under their purview. There are no scenarios in which the publisher or the original author of this work can be in any fashion deemed liable for any hardship or damages that may befall them after undertaking information described herein.

Additionally, the information in the following pages is intended only for informational purposes and should thus be thought of as universal. As befitting its nature, it is presented without assurance regarding its prolonged validity or interim quality. Trademarks that are mentioned are done without written consent and can in no way be considered an endorsement from the trademark holder.

Table of Contents

Book – I

Book – II

Book – III

Learn The Tricks While You Play!

Get this 3 part complete audiobook for <u>FREE</u> and get access to extra tips & tricks on scavenging, building, exploring, schematics and weapons never before released!!

<u>Download now for FREE</u> **and jump into the action!**

Visit this site: <u>bit.ly/FortnitePro</u>

Book – I

Fortnite:Battle Royale

Advanced Tips, Tricks, and Strategies from the World's Top Players to BECOME A PRO

Introduction

Congratulations and thank you for downloading *Fortnite:* The Ultimate Guide to Becoming a Pro in Fortnite Battle Royale.

The following chapters will discuss how you can quickly become an outstanding Fortnite player even if you're starting from next to nothing.

Fortnite: Battle Royale is one of the hottest games out there right now, and it seems like everybody is playing it. It's only natural that somebody would want to find a way to beat the competition and become one of the best. If you're looking for that chance, then this is the book for you.

Throughout these chapters, we're going to cover a lot of great information designed to take you from zero to hero in Fortnite.

There are plenty of books on this subject on the market. Thanks again for choosing this one! Every effort was made to ensure it is full of as much useful information as possible. Please enjoy!

Chapter 1: Transitioning from PUBG to Fortnite: Battle Royale

PUBG—PlayerUnknown's Battlegrounds—is yet another incredibly popular battle royale game. It was, in many ways, the first battle royale game to reach mainstream popularity when many streamers started to play it. As such, it wouldn't be too much of a surprise if PUBG were the first battle royale game that you've ever played.

If that's the case, then it's easy to be overwhelmed when you try to jump into Fortnite. The games are rather similar, but they also have a long list of differences between them which can throw off PUBG players, especially if they're more adept.

These differences are of significant importance to the overall logical flow of the game, though, and will have a rather large impact on the way that you play in general. So what are these differences, and how can you, as a PUBG player, transition to Fortnite with as few problems as possible?

The first thing that we need to get straight is probably something that you're going to recognize right away: Fortnite *looks* a lot different than PUBG. Where PUBG has very realistic visuals, Fortnite is based around being cartoony and plain silly. This can be somewhat charming once you get used to it in the same way that makes Team Fortress 2 a lot of fun.

However, with this comes a lot of gameplay changes. Where PUBG aims for realism, Fortnite does not strive towards any such thing. PUBG accounts for many more things than Fortnite does. For example, PUBG takes into account things such as bullet drop and bullet spread. Fortnite doesn't do this. Because of this, the gunplay in Fortnite is much simpler than the gunplay in PUBG. In Fortnite, the only guns which account for bullet drop are a select few sniper rifles.

Another aspect of gunplay which changes between the two is that Fortnite doesn't have a recoil system. This means that you will have to get used to its different system of aiming.

The largest difference between PUBG and Fortnite—and one which we'll talk about a lot over the course of this book—is the concept of building. Building is a huge part of Fortnite and plays a massive role in the way that the game plays out, in general. If you're coming from PUBG, then the idea of building will be pretty foreign to you.

We'll talk more in-depth about building later, but the thing you need to know is that much of Fortnite's defensive and proactive play revolves around building. For example, if you're being shot at, your best course of action is almost always to build a wall so that the enemy can't shoot you as easily. At the same time, the idea of gaining a height advantage through building is a major part of the strategy in Fortnite. Essentially, the overall strategy of the game changes quite a bit between the two, even if PUBG and Fortnite are both technically within the Battle Royale genre.

Yet another big difference between Fortnite and PUBG is that Fortnite doesn't have any cars—ones that you can drive, that is. If you're coming from PUBG, then you may have wondered how or where you can find cars. While you may have depended on cars in PUBG as an important defense resort, they simply don't exist in Fortnite in the same way.

This also comes down to another difference between PUBG and Fortnite: the latter has a much smaller map than PUBG does. This means quite a lot. For example, people are closer together, of course, and there is also no need for vehicles.

In terms of playstyle, the two games can also be rather different. In PUBG, many players choose to camp and play defensively. In Fortnite, however, the best play style is usually to be aggressive. Aggressive play is rewarded very well in Fortnite, as opposed to PUBG.

Defensive shooting isn't the name of the game in Fortnite. In PUBG, you may have developed the reflex of either shooting back or defensively retreating if you're being shot at. In Fortnite, the best course of action is to build defensive structures.

The inventory in Fortnite is smaller than the inventory in PUBG, and unlike PUBG, you cannot expand your inventory by finding a backpack. You'll need to, therefore, work on managing your inventory and building that skill. However, this becomes a lot easier the more you do it.

Chapter 2: Starting Out Strong

The first chapter was great if you already have some sort of background playing battle royale games. But what if you don't? This chapter will be focusing on building on what you already know so that you can start from scratch and then become a better player from there.

Let's start this chapter out with a simple question: What exactly *is* a battle royale game? The term is thrown around a lot and is used to describe far more games than just Fortnite. So what is it?

A battle royale game is one where a player is pitted against a whole lot of other players, usually 99, and then they fight it out to the death until only one player is standing. That player is then the winner of the match. Winning a match by yourself is referred to as *"soloing."*

In most battle royale games, you'll fly in above the map and then parachute down to some location on it. From here, you'll go start *loot*ing—finding weapons and other items across the map—and then start thinning the herd.

The strategy for battle royale games can run miles deep, and there's a lot more to it than I can really make clear in a short book. With that said, battle royale games—and Fortnite in particular—do have various general guidelines that you can follow to pick up the game pretty quickly and understand basic mechanics.

The first thing that you need to focus on is where you will drop in. Every game starts with you in the Battle Bus then skydiving onto the map below. The map is divided into several different sections, and knowing which one to drop to can make a world of difference.

Fortunately for you as a new Fortnite player, Fortnite generally does a good job of equalizing the quality of loot across the map. This means that in the purest sense, there isn't a "best place" to drop. However, some places are better than others for new players to drop. Tilted Towers, for instance, is highly recommended as a drop location for newer players.

Every place will have its own qualities. Places with more buildings have more loot, but there will also be more players there trying to kill you, and responding to this threat can be difficult for a new player to do. Tilted Towers has a lot of good loot and elevated locations so you can have a bit more protection than you would otherwise. Height advantage is extremely important in a game like Fortnite.

When you're starting out, the important thing to

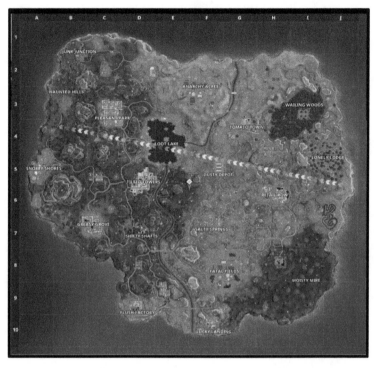

remember is the entire point of the game. You aren't playing a shoot 'em up. While the game is a *shooter*, its main goal is survival. Therefore, most of what you do should be to fulfill that goal: to be the last player standing. Survival implies playing both aggressively and defensively depending on the situation you're in. It will ultimately depend on the context of whatever is happening.

One of the most important assets to you as a new player is learning how to build well. For this, we've written a chapter a bit later in the book about how to build efficiently and effectively in Fortnite. However, for now, the important thing to know is that you can gather resources. This means using your tools to harvest materials around you. You can use these materials to build things and structures.

After you've gotten your loot to start out, remember that there's always more to get around the map. With time and experience, you'll get a better grip on where the loot chests are and what buildings/locations are good for your playstyle, as well as learning the weapons well enough to know what best suits your playstyle.

For most people, it's recommended that you have a weapon for each situation. This generally means a shotgun for close-range combat, an assault rifle for medium-range combat, and a sniper rifle for long-range combat or for picking people off from far away. You may not be able to find a sniper rifle easily, but you can find the others with relative ease, so be sure to just keep an eye out.

Your time should be spent gathering resources wherever you possibly can, moving throughout the map, and essentially trying to survive. For this reason, it's best to start playing Fortnite with friends. While it can be enticing to start playing solo and trying to win all on your own, if you're playing with friends, then it's much easier to handle the pressure of the unfamiliarity of the game along with the high-pressure nature of the game, especially as the game drags on and gets more intense. It can also make the waiting time between matches less of a drag if you die early.

So I mention the game getting more intense and stressful as the game drags on—why is that? Is there a reason? Well, yes. One major part of battle royale games is that the playable area of the map will eventually shrink. This is known as the *storm*. The storm mechanic was mainly intended, at first, to ensure that people didn't just camp in one place throughout the game and build up massive fortresses then just hold out there. The shrinking circle on the map is known as the *safe zone,* and the area outside the circle is known as the *storm.* When you are in the storm, you lose health over time, which is the primary motivator for moving within the circle when the time comes.

Note that as you venture around the map that noise is a huge deal in shooter games. Use this to your advantage. Whenever you're trying to loot somewhere or out in a field, be sure that you're listening closely and trying to hear if there are any enemies around. If so, then you have an important chance to get in the ready so that you have the opportunity to be fully prepared for whatever they may be planning to do.

On the other hand, you also need to be wary of the noise that *you're* making. People can hear you when you're bustling around and it may very well alert people to your position. Building can also create an exceptional amount of noise that can give away your position. Be aware of the noise that you make, because the fastest way to lose is to alert enemies of your location. Remember that Fortnite is a game about survival. Anything you do that hinders your chances of surviving is ultimately a poor, costly move. Moreover, the sound of movement in Fortnite is particularly louder than in other shooters, making the potential noise that you'll make a pretty major factor.

Fortnite is one of those games that's best learned through experience, but those are the best pieces of advice that I can give you for starting out strong and on the path to dominating Fortnite.

Chapter 3: Maximize Your V-Buck Rewards

V-Bucks are an important part of Fortnite. They allow you to get premium things in the game like purchasing llamas in the store which give you various perks in your gameplay for Save the World (Fortnite's other game mode). However, you can also use them to purchase various different in-game items in Battle Royale that will enable you to do new things or experience the gameplay in a slightly different manner. The weapons will also be cooler and more valuable. You can also use V-Bucks to do cool things like getting skins for your character and other things that will make your in-game experience more tailored to you.

So as you can tell, V-Bucks are definitely a highly desirable thing to have. As such, many players want to maximize the number of V-Bucks that they obtain. There are different ways for you to obtain V-Bucks.

The first point that I should make is that you need

to be careful to avoid V-Bucks scams where people offer to sell you V-Bucks, or where you install some sort of program to get "free" V-Bucks. If you do these, then you have a serious risk of losing your account if you're discovered, as well as potentially losing a good amount of money if you're asked to pay up front.

Therefore, we can pretty much take those options off of the table in terms of building up a long-term and steady manner of procuring V-Bucks. Unfortunately, there doesn't appear to be any sort of get-rich-quick scheme for getting V-Bucks aside from going ahead and buying them with real money.

Of course, this chapter isn't about how you can gain V-Bucks with *real* money. It's about how you can get V-Bucks through the various reward programs that are offered within the game itself.

The first and most obvious way to get V-Buck rewards is to reap the benefits of the daily login reward. While you won't get a ton of V-Bucks doing this, you're sure to make at least a little every day.

The more direct way to start earning V-Buck rewards is through the PvE mode, *Save the World*. In Save the World, you fight off hordes of zombies set out to destroy various structures in the game world. You do so on teams of with other people.

After playing through the story of Save the World a little bit, you'll unlock so-called *daily quests*. Daily quests are quests within Save the World that you can complete to get V-Buck rewards. Usually, these are pretty self-explanatory. You can get 50 V-Bucks per day by completing these quests.

You can also complete *Storm Shield missions*. Storm Shield missions are normal missions that are a part of the primary storyline of Save the World. Just by playing through these missions, you can earn about 100 V-Bucks each.

You can also gain V-Bucks by filling up your Collection Book. Throughout the game, you'll get things like schematics, heroes, survivors, and defenders that you can actually put in your book. Your Collection Book gains a little experience every time you add something new to it. However, note that when you consume something into your Collection Book, you can no longer use it. Avoid consuming legendary or epic items or any items that you particularly enjoy. You gain V-Buck rewards every time that you hit a certain level (6, 26, and 91 respectively.)

You can also do timed missions or events in Fortnite to gain more V-Bucks. Events are things which allow you to do quest lines to gain V-Bucks. You can gain a lot of V-Bucks just by working through these. Timed missions, on the other hand, are missions that will go away after a certain amount of time. Many of these will tell you their rewards and have relatively self-explanatory definitions. Do note that when you finish mini-boss missions, you can only get rewards from up to 3 per day (or 10 if there is a Blockbuster event going on). Any more would yield no rewards.

V-Bucks are a great asset within Fortnite, and

knowing how to get them and maximizing V-Buck rewards without spending a dime is important to a lot of people.

Chapter 4: Advanced Tips and Tricks

When you start playing Fortnite, there are some things that you can do that you may not realize you can do which you can use to boost your gameplay and become a better player in general. In this chapter, we're going to be going over a bunch of different tips and tricks that you can use to elevate your Fortnite play to the next level and start to massively overtake the other players that you'll run into.

Build to break a fall

This is a really obvious tip, but it's one that a lot of newer players don't realize. When you're falling, you can actually build mid-fall. Build floors into the sides of rocks and cliffs if you're falling to break your fall so that you take less fall damage than you would otherwise.

Don't miss the ammo crates

This is something that a lot of players don't take advantage of: there are a huge number of ammo crates scattered throughout Fortnite maps. Stocking up on ammo is important so that you can have more than enough to destroy the things that enemies build to defend themselves as well as actually killing them! If you neglect to open them, then you're going to be missing out in a major way.

Play against your opponent

This might seem like an obvious tip, but many newer players will actively fail to take this into account. The ability to tap into what your opponent is doing to outplay them is an absolutely crucial part of maneuvering in the context of Fortnite and ultimately winning more games.

How does one train the ability to start doing some impressive mind games? It all starts with the idea of recognizing and reacting. Think about what their next move is most likely to be and then move from there. You can often analyze the situation and anticipate their next move especially as you gain more and more experience with the game. Being able to read and analyze your opponents is a crucial part of becoming a better player. It's a skill that you'll inevitably build with time.

Part of it comes down to learning a lot more about the values of the materials that you're working with as well as seeing what other players are doing and then adapting to whatever they do. You'll learn quite a bit by observing, that is to say.

Shutting the Door

When you're playing battle royale games, whether it's Fortnite or something else, try to remember to close the door behind you when you enter through them. This will make it look like nobody has entered the building and lull people into a false sense of security. This puts you in a very advantageous position because you can take them by surprise when they come through. Alternatively, you can leave the door open, as an intimidating warning. The goal is to get in your opponent's head and make them think whatever you want.

Use Headphones

A big tip for you if you want to get better at
Fortnite is to start playing using headphones. If
you're playing on a console, then try to set up
either wireless headphones for your TV or console.
There are many options, and popular gaming
headsets for these will do the trick. We talked
earlier about how important sound is to Fortnite in
particular. Don't limit yourself by not allowing
yourself to hear everything going on around you.

Learn About the Metagame

This goes a bit along with the third tip. If you really
want to grow as a Fortnite player, you need to learn
to read and acknowledge the metagame. The idea
of a metagame extends beyond Fortnite and into
the domain of numerous other major competitive
games, even those that aren't virtual like chess or
poker.

What does *metagame* mean? Metagame refers to

the "game within the game". That is, the underlying concepts of the game that affect not just the game mechanics but the overall community, the picks of the game, the mindset of the game, and so on and so forth.

Metagame refers then to everything within the game that doesn't have to do directly with the game itself but rather exists around the game. For example, if a certain weapon or fort build is really popular, one could consider that part of the metagame.

The metagame also deals, however, with the idea of getting in your opponent's head. A favorite example to use is poker. In poker, the concept of a *poker face* could be seen as part of the metagame, because even though it's not an explicit mechanic of poker, the ability to hide your emotions and not have any tells is a very important part of being a successful poker player.

The Fortnite meta then is about what guns are most effective and what the best build paths and routes are. It's also about the things that you can do within the game in order to make your chances of winning better than your opponents' chances.

The most crucial parts of the metagame rest in what you can do to get in your opponents' heads and what you can expect them to do. Knowing the best courses of action in the game on an individual level, you can increase your chances of winning by both following those "best routes", as well as by using those in order to predict what your opponent is going to do and then outplaying them.

We already talked a bit about outplaying, but if you look into the actual Fortnite metagame and spend time watching major YouTubers and Twitch streamers playing the game, you'll learn more about what most players do, what *good* players do, and what *not to do*. You can also do a Google search in order to learn the Fortnite metagame really quickly. Some of it, too, is just going to come through practice and absorption, which is a bit of a shame.

In the end, the best way to learn the metagame is to recognize that it's there, which a lot of people never even do in the first place. Once you recog

Chapter 5: Build Better

As we've said multiple times before in this book, building is one of the most challenging and important strategic parts of Fortnite. If you want to be a good Fortnite player, then there's no better place to start than simply learning how to build well. Building has a whole lot of nuances, and the versatility of the things that you can build necessarily means that your building experience will be one of the major things that can take you higher.

In this chapter, we're going to explore a bunch of different tips that you can use to become a better builder and, in effect, a better Fortnite player in general. Hold on to your horses because this chapter will fly by.

Gathering Resources

In the second chapter, we talked about the importance of gathering resources in Fortnite. Resources are what allows you to build forts, protect yourself, and either play aggressively or defensively as necessary. One important thing that you need to keep in mind is that you're always going to be limiting yourself as a player if you try to exclusively get resources by staying in one place and doing what effectively amounts to nothing. When you do so, you leave yourself wide open, and that's not a good thing. Staying in one place doing nothing significantly raises your chances of getting caught.

Instead, you need to try to place emphasis on gathering materials while you move around the map. Gathering materials while you move ensures that you don't leave yourself vulnerable in any major way.

Building a Recon Fort

Building recon forts is one of the most essential and basic things for any Fortnite player to learn. A recon fort is essentially a small fort with walls around it. You build it by placing four walls around you and then jumping and placing a ramp below you. The ramp allows you to retreat as well as to peek out and over the fort.

You can also scale it up by building additional levels and a floor below you on top of the ramp. You then build a ramp on top of that flooring. This allows you to gain a height advantage even in the countryside very easily.

Building recon forts is an incredibly important defensive play that will allow you to quickly and easily gain some sort of defensive advantage compared to people who *don't* have a recon fort in a wide open space.

Add a Campfire to Your Fort

Campfires are wonderful things defensively because they allow you to heal up a little bit. However, they tend to be pretty obvious or take up important space. So what can you do instead? You can actually put a campfire below your ramp when you build it. This allows you to heal up even while you keep watch of what's going on around you.

This is important tactically. Health is, without a doubt, your most valuable resource in a game such as Fortnite. Consider how in any video game you play, an important part of it is, in one sense of another, the idea of slowly draining your opponent's available resources so that they have nothing to work with. If you lose health, you lose your most valuable resource. Having a way to stealthily gain that back in defense is important.

Ramp Tunnels

The truth about Fortnite is that being able to get higher will usually be the thing that lets you get an advantage. We talked about this in a basic way, but we didn't really build onto it from there.

Getting up to a higher point is crucial, so having a quick and efficient way to get higher up is also crucial, especially if that way can also be demonstrated to be safe and can protect you from one side to another.

The first thing that you do is build a wall. From there, you place a ramp going off the bottom of the wall and a ramp going off the top of the wall.

Therefore, the wall acts a bit like an anchor.

From here, you can add more ramps to the top and bottom and move up in your tunnel to get higher faster than you would be otherwise. This is especially useful when there is no safe or obvious way up, and you've looked around to ensure that the coast is clear from the exposed side.

Know How to Edit Your Structures

In Fortnite, you can actually edit your structures. This is important because when the game hits crunch time, you usually aren't putting a ton of thought into exactly what you're building. You tend to just build the first thing that you can to protect yourself. This can create some really wonky structures that don't have immediate purposes for a lot of their build decisions.

You can mitigate this problem by learning the things that you can do to the structures you build to make them serve new purposes. For example, if you were to remove the middle space from some wall that you've built, you'll actually create a window. This will allow you to peek out and get shots at your opponents.

You can also break a hole in a floor that you've built to do a ninja-esque jump scare attack. That will leave them confused and, more importantly, probably dead.

On top of that, you can do things like add a backdoor to your fort and then get out that way, which can really easily get you out of some sketchy situations.

Editing your structures allows you to find a lot of ways to creatively problem-solve your way out of a lot of situations that you may find yourself in.

Remap Your Keys

This one may seem obvious, but a lot of people leave out this really easy and intuitive option. The fact is that the keys for building aren't very easy for most people to reach. While you can use certain keys to scroll through the different options, this simply won't do when you're in the middle of a heated battle.

So what can you do instead? Simply remap the

building keys that are much easier for you to reach without even moving your hand. Do whatever you can that feels more natural than what is already there. This will allow you to build more effectively and efficiently at times where millisecond reactions count.

Plan Your Buildings and Resources

Don't waste your resources. This should go without saying, but it's easily overlooked. While things like wood aren't hard to come by in Fortnite, every resource is valuable and having the material to build an extra ramp could easily mean life or death.

Moreover, when you're in the early game, you aren't going to want to waste your own time building super complex or chaotic structures. This is because the map will shrink as the game goes on anyway. Be sure that you save resources for the structures that you're going to actually need them for, like those end of the game buildings that you need to save your neck.

Speaking of which, be sure you're planning ahead and obtaining resources like brick and stone so that when the end of the game comes, your forts have a little bit more staying power. Otherwise, the enemies will just be able to blast right through your forts, and that's definitely not an enviable position to be in. Just do what you can to be able to build better and stronger structures when that time comes around.

Chapter 6: Solo Successfully

Fortnite is an extremely fun game to learn and play with your friends. However, when you start trying to play it solo, it gets a lot more difficult. Moreover, when you're playing by yourself, you don't really have *anybody* to rely on. This means that there isn't anybody to keep watch of your bad habits and ensure that you're playing the best that you possibly can.

In essence, the onus of proper play is put completely on you. Your mistakes are entirely your own to realize and make. However, in this chapter, we're going to be talking about things that you can do to make your play better and become better at playing solo. There are a lot of different things that you can do to improve your general gameplay. This chapter will be focusing on tips and tricks that will help you massively improve your play.

The first thing that you need to do is to pay attention to where you find loot chests. Loot chests will often spawn in the same place, and while the loot itself isn't always the same, the location is rather consistent. Many people have read The Hunger Games or watched the films; you can really easily draw a parallel between the loot chests at the beginning of the game and the cornucopia in the books. Whoever gets the best loot first has the best chance of winning

The next thing that you need to do is to remember that pretty much everything is a building resource. This can be especially important when you're just starting out. The primary building materials in this game are wood, brick, and metal. Always look out for things that you can harvest for building materials, especially during the mid-game.

Another thing that's important is to remember to stay calm in any given fight situation. It's really easy to freak out and start playing sloppily when you see another player who has the potential to take you out. However, this isn't going to win you any skirmishes! Remember that you can only win if you stay alive.

Every fight has a linear nature, and there's always a better course of action that you can take to make your chances of winning a duel even better. Many of these will come more intuitively as you play more and learn the game more. Being able to recognize and take these courses of action ensure that you set yourself up for victory.

One of the most important tips in any shooter—not just Fortnite—is that you're vulnerable whenever you need to reload. If you find yourself running out of ammo on your current weapon, just switch to another weapon to finish them off. If you can't or don't want to do that, then try to find/build cover so that you have a little breathing room while you reload. This isn't such a big deal when you aren't soloing because your friends will cover you, but if you're on your own then you need to be aware of this.

Also, remember that you don't have to kill everybody to win. If you're not sure that you can actually kill somebody or can set yourself up advantageously in a duel, then don't bother shooting. Watch them for a moment and analyze their movements if they aren't aware that you're there. If they move around sporadically and don't know you're there, then it's best just to avoid letting them know of your presence.

A general tip for Fortnite is that when bullets go by, they bullet trails. This will help you figure out exactly where they may be coming from. With so many people on a map, being able to track down where these things are happening is crucial! It can save your life, so be attentive.

One tip for soloing is to take advantage of the storm. If you stay on the edge of the storm, you can leave the storm and then shoot from outside the storm towards the inside, allowing you to pick people off. A lot of variables play into this, though, and this technique will not always be a good one.

Try to avoid the storm if you can. This will ensure that you have as much health as possible and stay ahead of the curve. Unless, of course, your strategy specifically calls for usage of the storm.

When you're soloing, you need to remember that people don't have your back. What this means is that if you hear people or gunshots nearby, you need to take a second to analyze the situation. Remember that if you go waltzing into the situation, there could easily be a lot more people than you are actually ready to face, and you could end up dead in no time at all.

Soloing is hard, but once you get the hang of it, you start winning more. Winning all on your own can be really addicting because it means that you outwitted 99 other people. That is a very good feeling!

Conclusion

Thanks for making it through to the end of *Fortnite*: The Ultimate Guide to Becoming a Pro in Fortnite Battle Royale. Let's hope it was informative and able to provide you with all of the tools you need to achieve your goals, whatever they may be.

The next step is to start playing. Use these tips and strategies to become a great Fortnite player. I can sit here giving you tips and tricks all day, but they're absolutely worthless if you don't try using them!

Finally, if you found this book useful in any way, a review on Amazon is always appreciated!

Book - II

Fortnite: *Battle Royale*

The Ultimate Guide to Improve Your GUNPLAY AND SECRET BUILDING with Hidden Chests and more!

Introduction

Congratulations on downloading *Fortnite* and thank you for doing so.

The following chapters will discuss the most important tips and tricks for becoming a Fortnite pro. Even if you're starting from nothing, this book has something for you. It's going to cover a ton of super crucial topics that beginners always seem to overlook, and also address some things that only pros know about the game.

By the end of this book, you'll have a whole lot of fresh insight about how Fortnite works and how you can become a fantastic Fortnite player in no time flat. If you use the tricks and tips in this book, you'll have superior routes to everybody else, a great sense of game pacing, and a generally fantastic understanding of the game itself.   So what are you waiting for? Let's get started!

There are plenty of books on this subject on the market, thanks again for choosing this one! Every effort was made to ensure it is full of as much useful information as possible, please enjoy!

Chapter 1: 5 Unknown Tips that will Help You Win in Fortnite Battle Royale

There are a number of tips that only pros seem to know. This is good for you, though! We're going to start this book off by going through five different tips that pros abuse frequently. A lot of them may even seem like common sense, but chances are that you've never thought of them before.

Tip #1: Be Consistent

A lot of new players or people who simply play casually don't really acknowledge the value of both consistency as well as muscle memory. However, muscle memory is a very real thing. If you consistently slot your inventory in a certain way, then you're far more likely to go for the right thing in a fight.

The simple fact is that Fortnite is a game where reaction times matter, so the fraction of time that you spend fiddling around looking for the right weapon for the job can be a major drag and can actually end up losing you a fight. Avoid putting yourself in this situation: be consistent in your inventory slotting.

Tip #2: Remap Your Building Keys

This is another thing that a lot of people neglect to do. Building is such a major part of Fortnite, and if you ever watch professionals or high-profile streamers play the game, the chances are that they have rebound their building keys long ago.

This is because the building keys are by default a little bit out of the way and pretty hard to get to. This somewhat builds on tip 1's general idea: in a game where reaction times matter, the split second that it takes to reach up on the keyboard can make an incredibly huge difference.

Tip #3: Don't Move While You Shoot

This may seem counterintuitive. In a lot of games, it's a good idea to keep moving while you shoot, and indeed a major part of Fortnite's strategy rests in always moving around no matter what. However, a lot of people don't realize that if you don't stand still while you shoot, you actually drop a lot of accuracy on your shoots and it becomes a whole lot harder to hit people when you need to.

So basically, if you're firing anything but a shotgun, you need to be staying put when you shoot. You also should crouch in order to shoot whenever the opportunity presents itself.

Tip #4: Always Use Headphones

Fortnite is hugely based around sound, and all of the good players use headphones even if they don't play on PC. Fortnite's footstep sound effects are louder than they are in most other shooting games, and you can also depend on sound for things like hearing when somebody is building in the distance or when a gunfight is breaking out near you.

Whether or not you're a PC player, it's impossible to understate the importance of using a pair of headphones for the best gaming experience possible. Many more casual players don't play with headphones at all, so simply using this to your advantage will give you a major edge over a lot of the people that you'll be playing against.

Tip #5: Take Advantage of the Safe Zone

There is one surefire way to predict how people will be moving, and that's the storm. If you're not totally familiar with what the storm is, the storm is the area outside of the slowly shrinking circle which causes you to lose health if you stay within it. It was originally implemented as a way to get people to collapse toward the middle of the map instead of staying out in the edges and camping the whole game. We'll talk more about the impact of the storm later on in the book.

You can predict where people will be flocking from and where fights will be happening based on the way that the storm is shrinking. For example, if the shrinking circle is offset toward the top of the map, then that means the bottom of the map will be surrounded with the storm. This means that a lot of people who are concentrated on the bottom of the map will be flocking north, thereby meaning that a lot of fights will be happening along the southern edge of the storm.

You can use this sort of information in order to

keep yourself safe by maneuvering away from the offset so that you don't wind up in the middle of the firefights. A lot of people fail to take this sort of metagame strategy into account, which means by following this advice that you'll be ahead of the curve.

With that, we've covered five relatively unknown tips that can help you get ahead of the competition in Fortnite.

Chapter 2: Complete Guide to All Locations on the Map

Fortnite has a pretty intimidatingly large map. While it isn't as large as, say, PUBG's, it still is very large. What's more is that your decision about where to drop and where to go can have a massive impact on whether you win or lose a given game. The best players know the Fortnite map like the back of their hands and have their own strategies for when to go where and what to do there. Why should you be any different?

In this chapter, we're going to be going through all of the locations in Fortnite, including the new locations added in season 4. We're going to be break down every place in Fortnite so that you can have a good idea of what to expect at every one of them.

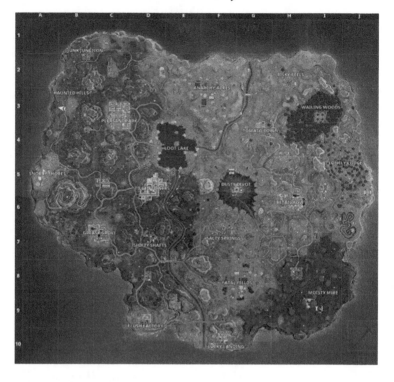

Anarchy Acres

The first location on our list is a pretty great place to start. It's secluded, and there's a motel that you can break into for a bunch of easy loot. Anarchy Acres is a fun little countryside that has a smattering of houses too. Be sure to check everything here because it's a pretty fantastic place to start your route. You can't go wrong by going to Anarchy Acres. Do be aware, though, that it's pretty open, which could make you an easy target - and you almost certainly aren't the only person who has decided to start their route with Anarchy Acres.

Dusty Divot

Between season 3 and season 4, there was a storyline wherein a meteor crashed right into the middle of the Fortnite map. What used to be known as the Dusty Depot would then be reduced to rubble, known as the Dusty Divot. In the middle of the Dusty Divot is a research station that you might wish to check out.

Moreover, in Dusty Divot, you'll find meteor remnants called Hot Rocks. This make it so that you don't take any damage from falling and also allow you to jump higher than you normally would.

Fatal Fields

Here is yet another countryside that you can venture around. While it's not as rich as Anarchy

Acres in terms of chest and loot potential, there are a bunch of other useful things to be found here. You can look in the houses and under this area's bridge, too, where you're likely to find a loot chest.

One of the best things here is that there are a ton of cars that you can break down with your pickaxe for their scrap metal. Metal is a super important resource later in the game, so be sure that you're picking it up wherever you can. Overall, this isn't necessarily a must in your route, but it isn't a bad inclusion either.

Flush Factory

This here is an industrial area full of factories. There is a ton of loot to be had in this area, but that isn't necessarily a good thing. You don't want to be one of the first people in this location, most likely. People like to start their routes here because of how many resources it has, so it's best to put this a little bit later in your route.

Don't worry, though; even if you don't prioritize it

and put it first, there's still a great chance that there will be plenty left for you. This is the kind of place that you don't want to miss in your route, so try to integrate it one way or another. Being there at the start of the game is dangerous, though.

Greasy Grove

This is a cute little neighborhood. It has a gas station and a restaurant for you to visit and pillage in addition to a bunch of different homes. While all of these give you a great chance to get some loot, you can also be sure that you will run into quite a lot of people here, so you may not want to start here.

It's not an essential on your route, but it's not *not* worth going. Leave that to your own discretion. Be warned, however, that if you do pay a visit to Greasy Grove that the restaurant tends to see a lot of people in it early on in the game, so bear that in mind if you do decide to go. You run a risk of early elimination if you don't play it smart.

Haunted Hills

You can find Haunted Hills near Junk Junction and Pleasant Park, but it's quite different from either of them - as you'll see pretty clearly if you start rummaging within it.

The mausoleum at Haunted Hills provides a place that's definitely worth hitting up if you find the chance. There are a few chests inside that you can dig around for, and there aren't likely to be many people here. However, there aren't many people here for a pretty good reason - it's on the very outer rim of the map, so looting here requires that you keep good watch of the circle. You don't want to be caught out in the middle of nowhere being forced to run back to the middle of the map.

With all of that said, Haunted Hills does provide an excellent place for you to scope people out from if you have been fortunate at this point to have grabbed a rifle, so do consider that if you should be so lucky as to find one.

Junk Junction

This place has a ton of materials. While there isn't a whole lot of comparatively good ammo or loot to be had, this still is an excellent starting point in terms of collecting resources. You will find a particularly large amount of metal here amongst thanks to all the cars, as well as a few other materials too. While it's not the best place to thin people out nor to find loot, it's still a great place to hit in order to mine out some metal for the late game, so consider it!

Lonely Lodge

Playstyles can differ a lot in Fortnite and are as unique as every individual player. Some people choose to focus themselves more on the idea of simply surviving through to the end of the game. If this is your end goal, then it's hard to find a better starting point than Lonely Lodge.

First off, it's a relatively quiet area to start out at. It's secluded and not a lot of people will be coming back this way generally. There is also a huge amount of loot for you to pick up here amidst the scattered huts and hovels. Beyond that, there's a really tall guard tower that you can head back to in order to firstly get some extra loot and also to thin people out should they decide to start heading in your direction. Getting domination over this area of the map can ensure a pretty strong early game for you. Do be wary, though, as it's on the edge of the map and the circle will close up on it fast. Retail Row is also near, so you can hit that as well during your route, but be careful if you do since it's a very high-activity spot.

Loot Lake

This one is pretty self-explanatory. In the middle of this lake area, you'll find a massive mansion. This is just as great of a landing as it implies, but it does have a drawback: this place draws a *lot* of players. So unless you know what you're doing, you have a great chance of getting knocked out fast.

However, if you do manage to poke your head

around here, you're likely to find a bunch of great materials and loot. There are as many as four chests in the mansion alone, and the areas around the house will have loot pretty often as well.

Moreover, if you land here and then have to get to the main area, you run a high risk of being killed since you'll be really vulnerable. That said, if you do manage to make it out, you'll do so with a ton of loot. I personally don't recommend landing here if you can avoid it.

Lucky Landing

Lucky Landing is a beautiful zone that's relatively small. It's not a great place to land because there's not a whole lot of loot to be had here. I'd recommend leaving it out of your route, because there simply won't be enough. Also, since this area is so small there's a pretty great chance that you'll be close to some enemies, so be aware that it's really risky.

Avoid Lucky Landing at all costs.

Moisty Mire

This area is altogether really underrated. Very few people come here because it's hard to navigate since you get slowed down so much in it. However, with that said, it somewhat works out to your advantage, especially if you know how to play smart. There are a ton of resources to be had here that can help you get off to a better start, especially wood.

You also have a relatively high chance of getting some good loot from chests as well. There's not going to be much of anybody around, so you can pretty easily survive your gearing-up period without a whole lot of trouble.

Pleasant Park

Pleasant Park has a lot of loot scattered amongst all of the houses, and it's relatively small too. You can make a run of this section of the map and make it out fairly fast while being pretty well geared up.

If you decide to land here, land on top of the gas station. If you do so, you can use your vantage in order to look around and see where enemies may be. From here, you can figure out exactly where you're wanting to go.

Retail Row

Retail Row offers a huge amount of areas to get geared up fast. It's in the center of the map, so you don't have to worry about the circle shrinking on you. However, on the other hand, it's an extremely popular area, so you do have to deal with that in the process. Try to land here first, if you're going to, and then get geared and get out as quickly as possible. You can also mine the cars in the area for valuable metal resources.

This place shouldn't be considered for the middle of your route. However, if you feel confident getting around other players, then you can place it at the start in order to get quick gear. If you do decide to land here, then you should also be taking into consideration the fact that you probably ought to land on top of the roof of a house in order to get to the loot within quicker.

Risky Reels

This is yet another new place that was added in at the start of Season 4. This section of the map is located near Anarchy Acres which we talked about earlier. It's another place dipped into the earth from a meteor strike.

Risky Reels is based around a drive-in theater that has been pounded into the center of the Earth. There are a number of vehicles that you can mine for their metal in the middle and a little bit of loot. It's not a top-priority location but it's not the worst to hit in the middle of your route.

Salty Springs

Salty Springs is yet another little town on the map, and it's near the middle of the map which means that you don't have to worry about the storm popping up any time soon and ruining your fun.

Also, there's a water tower in the middle of the town which allows you to get a height advantage and start sniping people from above. If you do this, you will gain a pretty serious advantage over everybody else in the game and be able to thin out the herd from a pretty solid vantage. You also gain a lot of security doing this because from this high up position, you'll be able to see if people decide to close in from here. You also will have a solid view of the lot of the map, which means you're in a favorable position to clear out enemies from even super far away.

Shifty Shafts

Shifty Shafts is relatively near to Tilted Towers. This place has a ton of loot for you to grab in its numerous tunnels and structures, so don't be afraid to come around here and go looking for them.

However, if you do go here, be aware that there are

a lot of turns and you're in a vulnerable position from behind in the claustrophobic tunnels. You can also use this to your advantage, though, by setting up for ambushing another player. Additionally, you want to be sure that you're using weapons meant for short ranges, like shotguns.

Snobby Shores

This is the area of the map where the rich people live, and because of this, there are a ton of houses with equipment for you to loot at your leisure. Pop in here and then try to get into their piles of loot. There also is an underground shelter with chests to be found near the house with a flat roof. Break through the floor of the house and you'll be in a bunker. This is a pretty safe place to get some loot because people who don't know the game terribly well normally have no idea that this location exists.

Snobby Shores is also somewhat naturally set up for defensive play thanks to its fencing and numerous structures, so if you find yourself up against enemies, you have a pretty solid chance of being able to outplay them.

Tilted Towers

There is, hands down, no location on the map so popular for landing as Tilted Towers. It's an extremely popular location with a ton of loot and tall buildings. With so much to get and so many opportunities for offensive play and height advantages, it's no wonder that most players choose to pop into Tilted Towers at the start of their game.

If you aren't as familiar with Fortnite, you'll likely want to stay away from Tilted Towers. There will be a whole lot of people here and you'll have to survive through a lot of fights. While this isn't such a big deal to a more experienced player, for new players all of the activity can be overwhelming.

If you do decide to head to Tilted Towers, then you'll find a number of chests and ammo crates scattered throughout the rooms in the towers. Additionally, you can pop by the gas station which has a secret tunnel where there's normally loot hidden.

Tomato Town

This place is a little bit underrated. Tomato Town is just another small town that has a restaurant as well as a gas station for you to break into and loot. It's up near Anarchy Acres and Dusty Divot so you can't go wrong with popping by on your route if your route starts near Anarchy Acres anyway. You don't want to linger too long because there isn't much to be had, but not many people pop by here and so it's a great place to harvest some vehicles for scrap metal as well as poke your head around in the restaurant and gas station for some crates. Normally, there's a crate behind the counter in the restaurant and one in the gas station as well.

Wailing Woods

This is the last major location that we're going to have to cover on our list. Wailing Woods is a heavily wooded area that makes an incredible area for defense, but can also be extremely easy to get lost in so be wary of that.

In the area, you'll find a broken-down house. Enter; this home's basement will normally have a fairly large amount of gear and ammo for you. Not many people pop around here early, so you can scour the house as well as the shipping crates a bit to the south with minimal stress. When all is said and done, you should be pretty well geared up and ready to move on to the next area in your route.

With that, we've covered all of the major locations that you need to know about in Fortnite. Hopefully at this point you have a somewhat better idea of the places you should most likely be hitting on your route and may even be forming some idea of a route in your head.

Chapter 3: Scoped AR vs Bolt-Action Sniper - Which One Should You Take?

Both the scoped assault rifle and the bolt-action sniper offer a pretty great long-distance choice. So what actually makes the difference between these two? Which one should you end up picking if you're trying to pad out the long-distance slot in your inventory?

Both guns have their own perks as well as their own drawbacks. This is a result of balance. The first thing you need to understand is that most guns in the game are *hitscan*. What this basically means is that most guns in the game damage their target as soon as they hit them. It's not based on *projectile* bullets but rather immediate damage based on your crosshair. If your crosshair is on the enemy, then the shot registers and your damage is counted.

Sniper rifles, on the other hand, are projectile-based. Like a real gun, too, there is a degree of *bullet drop*, which means that your bullet will actually drop over the distance that you're trying to shoot it just like it would in real life. This means that sniper rifles are very much harder to hit with than scoped ARs or really any other gun are. Combine this with the fact that sniping itself can be pretty difficult and require a lot of patience and you have a pretty tough gun to use.

However, it most definitely pays off for the diligent sniper. Using a bolt-action rifle, if somebody doesn't have shields then hitting them *anywhere* on the body will kill them, equalling out to about 120 damage even with a common gun. Landing a headshot with a bolt-action will kill somebody even *if* they have shields. There's nothing that can stop a headshot from a sniper rifle.

Compare this to scoped ARs. Scoped ARs are far easier to hit with than the bolt-action is, but they take a huge amount more shots than the sniper rifle does to kill somebody. For example, if somebody were walking around with full shields, you would have to hit them nine times with a scoped AR in order to kill them. By that time, they've likely already constructed a fort or started evading.

In the end, I would say that you most definitely should take the sniper if you can get your hands on one. As a new player, it will be hard to use them. Bullet drop is really difficult to account for, especially if you've never played a game with bullet drop in it before.

This pays off in the end, though. Once you get over the pretty steep learning curve, you actually have yourself an extremely effective weapon. You also pick it up pretty quickly despite it being really hard initially.

Given the choice between a bolt-action sniper rifle and a scoped assault rifle, I would say that you should most definitely take the scoped assault rifle.

Chapter 4: Tips to Improve Your Gunplay in Fortnite Battle Royale

In a game like Fortnite, shooting is everything. Your ability to handle your gun well and shoot accurately can make the difference between winning and losing and, ultimately, dying or surviving - which is what the whole struggle of Fortnite is all about.

This chapter is going to discuss things that you can do in order to build your skill with the guns in Fortnite. By the end of this chapter, you'll have a solid idea of the different things that you can do in order to become better with shooting and dominate duels.

The first thing that you need to do is challenge yourself. If you throw yourself into the fire, you'll slowly start to become better. I say slowly, but this is actually the *fastest* way to make real improvement. The way that I'd suggest doing this is going into squad mode but queueing up alone.

Then go into heavily populated areas. Squads will be trying to take you out and it's you against a bunch of teams. You're going to get absolutely decimated, but along the way you're going to learn to use your gun in the high pressure scenario and you'll become a much better shooter in general.

Always remember to aim instead of firing from the hip. This can make such a colossal difference it's not even funny. Your accuracy while aiming instead of hip firing absolutely shoots up in a way that's hardly even measurable. Practice finding your targets quickly while aiming and then building that skill.

One way that you can build this skill is to load into a game and then go somewhere secluded in the game. Grab a gun and then just play by yourself. Your intent here isn't to win; it's just to practice hitting still targets in the distance. Eventually, you can try working your way up to moving targets and other people, but this will help you get your bearings and also help you quickly locate whatever is in your sights after aiming.

A tip that a lot of pros suggest is to lower your sensitivity. You can do this regardless of platform, though if you're playing on mobile you may actually wish to turn your sensitivity up if you haven't gotten used to it yet. A lower sensitivity makes it far, far easier to aim where you're wanting to. However, this has the trade-off of not being able to move in your sights as quickly, so evaluate whether or not this is worth it to you.

One major difference between Fortnite and a lot of shooting games is that Fortnite has a recoil mechanic. You will need to learn to account for this mechanic in your gunplay training. Recoil causes your crosshair to be off for a brief second after firing, much like it would with a real game.

Don't move and shoot, ever. This massively lowers your inaccuracy. The best ways to improve your accuracy are to stop what you're doing, stand still, and crouch down. If you do this, then you can trust that your bullets are most likely going to hit. You can also improve the accuracy of your bullets by using higher rarity guns, but you're likely going to do this anyway.

If you're playing on a console, then auto-aim can be a major pain. However, it can also be a major help. Many players of console versions have complained that auto-aim can throw off their aim and cause the bullets to shoot inaccurately and nowhere close to where they're wanting them to hit in the first place. In order to account for this, always let auto-aim recenter when you're playing on console before you shoot. This will give the game time to adjust. Some people say that if you have a rough time hitting accurately on consoles, it isn't entirely your fault; I'd have to agree with that assessment. The best way to ensure your accuracy is to not play on a console but rather to play on PC where you have full control and can turn off auto-aim. However, in lieu of this option, you're going to just have to navigate auto-aim unfortunately.

Learning how to properly use your guns and shoot with accuracy is an essential part of becoming a solid Fortnite player, so I'm not at all surprised that you're interested in that. Hopefully this chapter has helped you learn the best strategies for improving your gunplay.

Chapter 5: Tips to Let You Land on the Ground Faster in Fortnite Battle Royale

Landing fast is extremely important in Fortnite. The faster you land, the greater your chance of getting to supplies before anybody else does, and the better your chances are of surviving the early game since there are less people to give you trouble.

This chapter is going to be about all the things that you can do in order to speed up your landing in Fortnite and get on the ground moving as quickly as possible.

If you try to jump out directly above wherever you want to land, then you're just going to be slowed down by your parachute. Instead of trying to jump directly above it, you should instead try to dive towards an area that is *close* to where you want to land. From here, you can just head in the general direction that you're wanting to go by gliding.

Next what you're going to want to do is deploy your parachute once you're *close* to the ground then glide over to where you want to go, which will keep you from just slowly floating down to it.

When you jump, start immediately pressing forward in order to land faster. Let your parachute eventually deploy on its own.

It may seem like a good idea to try to jump above something high, but this actually works in the opposite way. When you jump out over something that's high up, your parachute will deploy faster which leads to you actually being in the air longer than you normally would.

If you want to land faster, try jumping out over water. When you jump out over water, it throws the game off and causes your parachute to not deploy before you want it to. When you get sufficiently close to water, deploy your glider and then swoop up to where you want to be on the land.

This works significantly well, too, if you do it on the

edge of the map. There are a lot of buildings on the edges of the map that people tend to ignore, and these usually have a lot of great loot in them that can be all yours. Whether or not you decide to do that, though, you still should take advantage of the fact that jumping out over water keeps your parachute from deploying because you can use this to be on the ground before anybody else.

Landing faster is an immensely important part of Fortnite because it gives you a huge tactical advantage, so it's pretty necessary that you start practicing ways to actually land faster than anybody else.

Chapter 6: Item and Weapon Rarities in Fortnite Battle Royale

Things in Fortnite are coded based upon their rarity. This idea of rarity applies to both how common an item or weapon is, as well as how good its stats are. Things which are rarer both drop less often *and* have better stats than things which are less rare.

The rarities are coded as such:

Common items are coded as *gray.*

Uncommon items are coded as *green.*

Rare items are coded as *blue.*

Epic items are coded as *purple.*

Legendary items are coded as *orange.*

Mythic items are coded as *gold.*

Mythic rarity applies solely to special items that don't really pop up in Battle Royale mode, but because of how special and rare they are, it was worth mentioning them. Other than that, the rarities are ordered sequentially. So, for example, an epic item is much rarer than an uncommon item, and also rarer than a rare item.

You can find items of various rarities scattered throughout the map. Sometimes, rarities are going to impact your overall loadout decisions. For example, if you were to find a blue scoped AR, it still would be better than an epic scoped M16, because the scoped AR is a better gun than the M16 stats-wise.

Pay attention to these sort of discrepancies. For the most part, you'll pick them up naturally as you start playing the game more and more.

Chapter 7: What to Prioritize for Your Inventory and Playstyle in Fortnite Battle Royale

Fortnite is the sort of game where small things can make a really big difference. In this chapter, we're going to be going over two major different gameplay components that can impact whether you win or lose: *playstyle* and *inventory*.

First, let's talk about playstyle. What is playstyle? Playstyle refers to the manner in which you play the game. For example, you may have a more subdued playstyle where you tend to avoid people and just pick up resources and try to survive, or you may have more aggressive playstyle where you actively seek out fights.

Some games tend to prefer one or the other, and Fortnite is no exception. When you're playing Fortnite, you most certainly want to adopt a more aggressive playstyle. With that said, let's talk about what this means.

When I say that in Fortnite, you want to have a more aggressive playstyle, I don't mean that when you're playing Fortnite you want to go all out and attempt to take on every single fight that you can. That's a really good way to end up dead in no time flat, or at the very least constantly giving away your position.

However, there is an opposite to this playstyle which you really want to avoid: cowardice. It may seem counterintuitive since the whole goal of Fortnite is surviving, but you don't need to avoid taking on fights. It's through winning gunfights and thinning the herd that you will slowly start to emerge as the victor for a given match.

Another really important reasoning to this is that a lot of Fortnite comes down to your comfortability with the controls and your ability to have better mechanics than the enemy. Mechanics in the context of video games refers to your ability to overwhelm people with your raw knowledge of how the game works and the raw skills that you've built up while playing the game.

Much like anything else, one of the only ways to get better is to constantly challenge yourself, and the way to challenge yourself in Fortnite is by pushing the boundaries of what you can do and then learning from it when it doesn't play out. This isn't something that you're going to ever do if you're constantly avoiding people.

Additionally, once somebody engages a fight, there is still a chance that you can outplay them and win the duel, especially if you're managing your inventory well and you have a solid understanding of things like building.

Beyond all of that though, the simple fact is that playing too defensively just puts you at a major disadvantage in terms of the game. You will constantly be a target but will hardly ever be seeking out targets. It is possible to win a game of Fortnite without ever firing, but it's extremely rare. Don't try to do that. Just try to push yourself and learn the game more so that you feel more confident when you do play aggressively.

So in terms of inventory, what can you prioritize in order to ensure that you have the best game possible? There isn't quite a consensus on this, but there is a generally solid idea among the community of what you should have in your inventory. You only have five inventory slots, so what you decide to put in them really matters.

One thing that you need to have in your inventory is a close-quarters weapon. This necessarily means that you need to have a shotgun in your inventory ready to be used at any time. The importance of having something in your inventory that you can use in order to get up close and personal is extremely important. If somebody else has a shotgun and you only have an assault rifle then they are going to win that fight at anything less than 10 paces. Don't put yourself in that situation. Try to make sure that you have a shotgun. They're pretty common.

Another thing that you need to have is an assault rifle. Assault rifles are the go-to gun in Fortnite unless you're at close or far range. Most of the time, you'll be using this, especially out in the open. It doesn't quite matter what kind of assault rifle it is, but burst rifles are generally preferred to normal assault rifles, and you should always opt for a SCAR if you can. SCARs are without a doubt the best weapon in the game in most situations you'll encounter.

Next, you're going to want something else in order to add another offensive technique to your inventory. If you find yourself keen on sniping, then you should obviously probably fill this slot with a rocket launcher and try to thin people out from one of the safe vantage points on the map, a few of which we've talked about. Otherwise, you may want to use this slot for a rocket or grenade launcher, preferably the grenade launcher if possible. If you decide to take a sniper, you can refer to this book's chapter on which sniper rifle is the best.

You're going to want to use your fourth slot for holding your shield items. These are of the utmost importance because they're essentially a second health bar. If you never come across shields, you may as well pad this slot out with a fourth weapon or with extra health items.

Lastly, your fifth slot should ideally be those things which can boost your health like chug jugs and bandages. Do your best to keep this slot filled, because there is no understating how important being able to regenerate health is in the context of Fortnite. There really isn't anything so important.

With that, we've discussed what you should prioritize both in your playstyle and your inventory. I hope this chapter was conducive to helping you figure out just how you're going to play this game.

Chapter 8: The Complete Beginners Guide to Building

Building is one of the most important parts of Fortnite, so if you're trying to play Fortnite without a proper knowledge of how to build then you're going to quickly find yourself at a loss... or having losses.

Rest assured, this chapter is going to focus on how to start building basic structures and what building even is or can do for you.

Building is the thing which actually separates Fortnite from similar battle royale games such as PUBG. While there are many features that Fortnite shares with other battle royale games, it is building specifically which causes the game to stand out amongst the crowd.

Over the course of a game of Fortnite, you'll ideally be collecting resources. The term *resources* refers to wood, metal, and brick, all of which can be mined throughout the map using your trusty pickaxe. You need to be mining resources whenever you can because you are most definitely going to need them later.

Why? Because building is everything in Fortnite. It gives you options both offensively and defensively. If you want to be a good Fortnite player, you need to understand that a lot of the skill involved revolves around building.

Fortnite allows you to place things like walls and floors and ramps, as well as other various kinds of structures. After you place down a blueprint for these structures, building will commence. After a few moments, the structures will be considered built and you'll be ready to go.

Except, it's really not that easy unfortunately. The first thing you need to bear in mind in Fortnite is that building makes a *lot* of noise, and if you haven't noticed from what you've already played, noise is a huge deal in Fortnite. If you build at an inopportune time, then you could end up giving away your position to your enemies - which is the absolute *last* thing that you want to do.

One of the most basic structures that you can build is called a *panic fort*. You build a panic fort when you're preparing for a gunfight, like when you see an enemy approaching. In order to build a panic fort, you simply place three walls around you, then jump and place a ramp leading up to one wall. Then you play a wall where you hadn't placed it before so that you're boxed into the panic ramp.

You can escape back on the ramp for cover or come out to shoot, and when you do come out you have a considerable height advantage over the enemy.

If you jump again from on top of your ramp, you can place a floor below you and then build yet another story onto your panic fort. You can keep doing this over and over which will give you a major height advantage.

Note that panic forts aren't meant to be a permanent structure, they're a quick fix when you're about to be engaged upon. But they do provide an excellent example of some of the things that you can build in Fortnite. Building is a strategic thing, and it's a major part of the overall gameflow within Fortnite. You'll become a better builder as you go on, but it doesn't hurt to watch streamers or Fortnite YouTubers and observe what they do.

Chapter 9: The Secret Building Strategy Almost No One Knows About

In this chapter, we're going to be talking about a building strategy that can win you a ton of games. The best part about this strategy is that it seems like almost nobody knows about it!

Have you ever heard of the Stairway to Heaven? Chances are that you haven't. The Stairway to Heaven is a super simple way to win a game without ever really having to shoot anybody. You can spend the entire game chilling out above everything and everybody else completely on your own. Then the end of the game comes and boom, Victory Royale. So how do you construct a Stairway to Heaven?

It's actually pretty simple. You construct a Stairway to Heaven by landing in a very secluded area near the edge of the map; you may opt for Lonely Lodges, for example. Then you just start mining resources like wood and whatever else you can find. Loot as much as you can near you and focus on staying alive. If you can get your hands on a sniper rifle, then you're absolutely set... if not, you may be at a little bit of a loss, but you can still work with it. Your goal is to survive and, if you do this right, you're almost certain to make it to the end of the game.

So, with all of that said, once you have your materials mined and a decent gear set-up together, you need to get to work on the next part: building your Stairway. After about ten minutes, you should finally see the the circle of the map closing in toward you. Once it gets to pretty much exactly where you are, start building your staircase up into the sky. You should be able to just barely outpace the circle. Eventually, you'll be at the height limit. From here, you're now way in the sky above everybody else and you can put platforms pretty much wherever you want in order to get a solid vantage over the entirety of the playable area. Try to keep outpacing the circle as it expands inward.

If you do this right, you should end up being way

above everybody else playing the waiting game. Try to expand beyond just one-wide ramps in the sky so that you can have a little security if somebody see what you're doing and starts trying to kill you.

In the end, it'll hopefully come down to just you and one other person. At this point, you'll have had a free ride to the end game. From here, it's all pretty much on you and your building ability. If you get lucky, though, you should be able to snipe them with a sniper rifle from above and not have to worry about them, securing your way to a full on Victory Royale. Woo!

Chapter 10: 7 More Miscellaneous Advanced Tips

This chapter is just going to be based around some additional tips that you can use in order to better thwart the competition. Pay close attention because you can definitely use this to your advantage!

Wood over metal

This applies for any building material, really. Wood is most of the time going to be a superior choice to any other material in the game. The only exception is when it comes down to the end of the game and you're trying to construct your final fort.

Why?, you may ask. The answer is simple: while wood has a relatively low *final* health compared to materials like brick and stone, it does have a really high *initial* health compared to them. Other materials have to ramp up to their full potential, where wood builds quickly and is relatively strong from the moment you place it. It's also extremely abundant, so you're pretty much never going to run out of it.

As I said, this somewhat changes when you approach the end of the game. Then, you should have a bit more seclusion and planning time with which you can start to build a more permanent fort. You aren't at as much risk of people trying to tear down whatever you're building, and you also aren't *wasting* your stronger materials by trying to place them before they can do you much good.

Double your guns

Equipping two of the same type of weapon can be an extremely effective strategy. For example, you can wield two assault rifles in your inventory. When you would normally need to reload one, you simply switch to the other weapon of the same time and keep doing what you were doing.

This strategy can be extremely strong when used correctly and can easily win you several duels.

Move fast

There's no reason to dilly-dally in Fortnite, end of

story. You want to do two things: you want to *always* be moving (unless you're shooting!), and you want to always be moving *quickly*. Get resources as you move along, always try to get pop by chests and ammo crates, but don't linger in any area for too long. Otherwise, you leave yourself massively open to being taken out by an enemy.

Always build high

Height advantage is a huge deal in Fortnite. You always want to be building up. This will give you a greater advantage over your enemies and also force people to try to keep up with you, making them waste their resources and allowing you to stay one step ahead. Build upwards and not necessarily outward.

Never cut down entire trees

This one is really simple in concept, but it's important to remember. Try to avoid cutting down entire trees. This leaves a really obvious trail behind and lets people know where you've been. While you should constantly be mining them for resources, avoid letting people know that you've been around. You'll thank me later.

Build in order to save yourself

One of the most important things in Fortnite is building defensively. If you pay attention to people who are known for being really great at the game, they tend to build as a *reflex*. If they get shot at, they start building. Building is a huge defensive mechanism. If somebody starts shooting at you, plop down a wood wall. This breaks their line of fire and also lets you fake them out for a hot minute.

Another way that you can build to save yourself is by placing a floor below you when falling, especially off a cliff. The floor will break your fall and you'll end up taking far less fall damage. You can do this over and over. This also allows you a quick getaway down a cliffside once you've mastered this technique.

You can also, for example, build platforms in order to avoid going through a boggy marsh or through a lake, which would slow you down and leave you vulnerable. In the end, building isn't just for forts - it's for all elements of strategy within this game. Think of it like such and always be considering how you can build in order to save yourself.

Don't plan for permanence

In short, don't build elaborate structures early on in the game. Chances are that it's going to become irrelevant as the play circle shrinks thanks to the storm anyway. Make your early structures extremely disposable and mostly wood. Your focus in the early and mid-game needs to be gathering resources and looting throughout the map, anyway, as well as just generally staying alive. It simply isn't the time yet to set up camp somewhere. Fortnite does *not* reward that style of play.

With that, we've covered seven more advanced tips that can help you gain a massive competitive edge in Fortnite. If you incorporate these into your play, I promise that you'll start seeing immediate results.

Chapter 11: Controller Settings Advice

Some people aren't playing with a keyboard and mouse. Due to the nature of Fortnite, these people are at a bit of a disadvantage. Don't worry, though - this chapter is meant to help you set up the best controller layout that you can if you're playing on PS4 or Xbox One!

The main thing that may give you a little trouble is the fact that the standard sensitivity settings on controllers might be a little low for your liking. If you want to be more accurate, you're probably going to want to turn these numbers up so that you can aim better and be more able to move your view around when it counts.

In the controller settings menu, you'll first want to adjust is Controller X and Y Axis sensitivity. These control how quickly you're able to turn, so you're going to want to turn these up. This will enable you to respond faster to enemies near you and return fire more effectively. I would recommend that you set these at about 0.80 or 0.85.

You're also going to want to turn down your Gamepad ADS Sensitivity. This controls how fickle of a response the controller offers when you're trying to aim down the sights. You probably want this sitting at about 0.6 to 0.65 so that you can have a smoother aiming experience.

Lastly, you're going to want to turn up your scope sensitivity. This is pretty self-explanatory - it's the sensitivity of the scope when you're aiming through your sniper rifle. You can set this around 0.80 or 0.85 and probably have a good time.

There isn't a whole lot of customization to be done as far as controller bindings go, but there are some things that you can do in order to make your overall play experience better. Adjusting your sensitivity will pay off, trust me. It will be a little difficult to adjust to at first, but it will be worth it.

Chapter 12: What Everybody Needs to Know About Fortnite Battle Royale on Mobile

Fortnite has a mobile version, and there simply put, it's hard. It's a lot harder to play than its PC and console counterparts. However, there are some things that are implemented in order to balance the game out for those who are playing on their mobile devices.

Perhaps the most obvious difference between the two is that since the mobile version is being played on a touchscreen, everything needs to be firstly compressed but secondly controlled by one's fingers. Unfortunately, your fingers can tend to get in the way on small phone screens. This isn't such a big deal on iPad devices, however, where you have more screen real estate than you do on iPhones.

Either way, it's far from desirable in a game where being able to be aware of your surroundings is one of the most important parts of the overall game strategy bar pretty much none. This is worsened by the fact that a lot of the things that you would expect to be really intuitive from your experience playing on PC and console, like constructing things or choosing a certain weapon, are complicated by the touchscreen interface. Instead of just pressing a key, you have to seek out the relevant icon on screen and then press it in order to get the thing that you're wanting. This can be really difficult when you're in a tense situation like a gunfight or a duel.

In order to make up for these shortcomings, though, some things have been implemented in the mobile version of the game that serve to make it an easier and more fluid playing experience for people who are deciding to play on mobile.

Perhaps the most immediate and obvious is the fact that the aim assist on the mobile version is far more intense than the aim assist on the PC or console versions. This helps out quite a bit when you have to do more awkward motions in order to turn your character around.

Additionally, there are a number of visual nods that allow you to know when something important is near you. For example, if there are gunshots fired or footsteps coming from nearby, there will be an icon that indicates the direction that it's coming from. The visual nods will also help you to locate loot boxes.

In the end, though, the mobile version of Fortnite could be much worse than it is. It's actually fairly solid. You can play with people across any platform and not worry about whether they're playing on PC or console. This can be a good or bad thing; you may be at a disadvantage against people who are more skilled than you who are playing on a PC, but at the same time you may not have a "normal" gaming option and may find that the mobile version offers a really convenient way for you to just play with your friends without having to invest in a costly gaming rig. It also lets you get in your Fortnite no matter where you go without having to sacrifice quality or having to lug a gaming rig around.

Epic is continually updating their mobile version of Fortnite, so you can only expect that the mobile version is going to get better. It's easy to have a lot of questions about this; after all, jamming a PC game into a mobile device has hardly ever been done well, and especially hardly on the same servers that the same PC game runs on. But Epic Games have done it fairly well with Fortnite.

Aside from all of that, many things remain the same. Playing the game on a mobile device isn't so terribly clunky as to put one off. While it's not too easy, it could be much worse than it is. The game experience as a whole is pretty much the same aside from the small compensatory things that have been added to account for the natural awkwardness of the game on mobile.

For example, all of the weapons remain the same and the maps are essentially the same. On top of that, every update which gets pushed out for Fortnite on the PC and console versions is also pushed out to the mobile version, so you'll never be lagging behind your friends.

If playing on mobile is your only option for a given situation, then you could do a lot worse. While you can't realistically expect to be facing up against some of the best players in the world while playing on a mobile device, you can still expect a fun and enjoyable gaming experience. And in the end, isn't that simple idea - having casual fun - what a game like Fortnite is really supposed to be about?

Conclusion

Thank for making it through to the end of *Fortnite*, let's hope it was informative and able to provide you with all of the tools you need to achieve your goals whatever they may be.

The next step is to break out Fortnite and start playing. The only way to measurably improve is to actually apply these skills in the game and challenge yourself to get better. I could teach you all of the nifty tips and tricks in the world and it wouldn't matter if you weren't putting them to use.

Before this book comes to a close, I just want to note the importance of keeping a calm head in becoming a better player. In competitive games, especially games that get as tense as Fortnite can, it can be really easy to lose your cool. However, when you do this, you aren't accomplishing anything. You're only making it harder for yourself to get better and making it more likely that you perform badly by allowing yourself to get distracted.

Whenever you die in any game, regardless of what

it is but especially in Fortnite, always use it as a chance to reflect. What things did you do that you ultimately could have done better? Could you have managed your resources better, or all around handled the map better? Could you have been less aggressive, or could you have maybe been *more* aggressive?

All of these things are extremely important considerations in the overall context of becoming a better Fortnite player. You're only going to get better if you can be honest with yourself about when you mess up and then use those experiences to get better.

I sincerely hope that this book has helped you realize some crucial ways that you can become a better player. Finally, if you found this book useful in any way, a review on Amazon is always appreciated!

Book – III

Fortnite:Battle Royale

The Ultimate Guide – SECRET TIPS, TRICKS AND STRATEGIES That The Elite Players and Top Streamers Use to Win

Introduction

Congratulations on downloading *Fortnite Battle Royale* and thank you for doing so.

The following chapters will discuss how to quickly and effectively become a fantastic Fortnite player. We'll start from the very basics and then move up from there as we cover a myriad of different topics involving crucial things such as building, dueling, finding the best loot, and much more. You may start knowing next to nothing but by the end of this game, you're going to feel confident going forward with Fortnite.

There are plenty of books on this subject on the market, thanks again for choosing this one! Every effort was made to ensure it is full of as much useful information as possible, please enjoy!

Chapter 1: Top 9 Mistakes Beginners Make

In starting out this book, it's important that we pick a reasonable point to start *from*. In this light, it seems really reasonable to start by talking about the mistakes that most new players make a lot of the time. The thing is that there are many things which are easily preventable that could massively improve your gameplay experience if you were to avoid doing them. Just by learning from the things I talk about on this page, you will be on the path to being a much better player in general.

Tip #1: Starting Out Smart

It's hard to get better if your gameplay is doomed from the very start. The simple fact is that a lot of people will start out in Fortnite by trying to run towards a huge urban area. The bad side of this is that people will often be waiting, ready to take you out. The bigger cities simply aren't a great place to start out. This is where everybody goes, and some people are going to have weapons before you do. Some people are going to know the best places to be even better than you do. Your best bet, then, is to just avoid people as much as possible for the first couple minutes.

Why? If you start out the game by avoiding people and gathering resources and weapons at houses where people haven't visited yet, then you're much more likely to survive later into the game - especially when this is coupled with some of the other skills that we're going to be talking about in this book.

Tip #2: Failing to Set Yourself Up for Success

Equipping is a huge part of Fortnite. The weapons and resources that you find along the way will make or break your game. You can't expect to win if you don't take the time to set yourself *up* to win.

When you land on the map, the first thing that you need to focus on is stocking up. Fortunately, in this book, we're going to talk about some of the best places for looting. What's more is that as you play on and discover more about the game and get better at it, you'll start remembering the places where chests are most likely to pop up. While chests don't always spawn in the same place, there is some degree of regularity to their spawning patterns.

Tip #3: Failing to Collect Enough Materials

We'll be talking a lot more about building and the purpose that it serves later on in the book. For right now, though, we really need to drive home the importance of remembering to collect building materials as much and as often as you can.

Building materials are absolutely essential to the overall strategy of Fortnite, and neglecting to get them is pretty much not an option if you want to be a good Fortnite player. Don't forget to collect these crucial parts of the gameplay experience.

Tip #4: Failing to Use the Map Strategically

This seems like it might go without saying, but it's something that a lot of new players overlook. Don't forget that your goal in playing Fortnite is to *win*, and winning requires the use of strategy. Don't be afraid to use things such as the foliage around you and the natural terrain in order to give yourself an advantage.

For example, if there is a grove of trees on the top of a hill, or sets of rocks, or even buildings that are strategically placed, you can outwit other players and remain undetected.

A lot of the time, if you use the map strategically enough, you can allow yourself the opportunity to remain pretty much undetected at key moments of the game. The hard part will mainly be getting to these points where you can use the map strategically.

Tip #5: Running from Battles and Confrontation

A lot of people will overemphasise the importance of not fighting when they're playing Fortnite. They might think too hard about how they're trying to survive and will avoid giving themselves the opportunity to both thin out the herd as well as the opportunity to grow as a player.

It's almost impossible to win a game of Fortnite without shooting at all. While it is *possible*, it rarely ever happens. While the game *is* called <u>Fortnite</u>, it's not in your best interest to just build a fort and camp out the whole game. Don't just avoid firing at all because you may end up giving your location away. If you have a clear opportunity to kill somebody, then go for it. You have pretty much no reason not to, and you get their loot if you get a kill.

More than that, whenever you do get a kill on somebody, that's one less person that you have to worry about getting a kill on you. This definitely works out to your advantage! Don't be afraid to kill somebody if you have the opportunity to.

Tip #6: Fighting When You Don't Need To

This, however, can be an even bigger mistake that a lot of newer players tend to make. The fact of the matter is that Fortnite *is* a *defensive* and *strategic* game. Many people who are new to the game will make the mistake of playing way too aggressively. In the process, they'll often overextend themselves or make tiny mistakes that quickly lead up to them being dead and waiting for the next match.

Remember that every time you shoot, you make your position known - not just to the person you're shooting at, but also to anybody within earshot or who notices the tracer coming from your bullet. This is a fatal mistake that so many players make constantly, so it's imperative that you avoid making it yourself. It's important that you strike up some sort of balance between fighting too often and fighting too little.

Tip #7: Using the Wrong Weapon for the Situation

A lot of people will often stick to only one weapon, which is a pretty big mistake. While you can definitely get comfortable with the feel of a certain weapon, this can be a major drawback. It's a great gun, and it has a lot of versatility, but it isn't the best weapon all the time and if it's the only one you're using, you'll find yourself getting outgunned pretty easily.

For example, if you're in close quarters and you're up against somebody using a shotgun, they will do far more damage to you than you will to them. For this reason, if you're within a building or some other location where you'll be exceptionally close to opponents, you should be using your shotgun. If you're up against somebody who has closed themselves off, you should be using your explosives over anything else. If you are going up against somebody at a distance, you should use your sniper rifle. If you're in an open area or at a medium distance, then you should use your assault rifle.

Just get used to switching between your weapons and picking the right choice for the job. It can make a huge difference in duel situations.

Tip #8: Immediately Looting an Enemy

If you kill somebody, it can be extremely tempting to go pick up everything they dropped immediately. However, if you do this, you're putting yourself in an extremely dangerous situation. Instead of doing this, what you need to do is carefully review the situation, wait a moment, and see if there are any enemies around. It's easy to forget about the fact that you and the enemy's shooting will make a ton of noise, but they *do*, and they may be enough to alert other enemies who are nearby. Assume that there's always somebody nearby and give it a second. If you're lucky, they may come up and try to loot it, which gives you a clear shot at them.

Tip #9: Not Using Building Strategically

New players constantly underbuild. Building is one of the most important strategic factors in the entirety of Fortnite. We'll be talking more about this at length later on in the book, such as how to master the all-important panic fort or things of a similar nature. However, for now, the best thing to do is to pay attention to what YouTubers and streamers of Fortnite do; almost all of the time, if they're in a bad situation, they will generally build some sort of cover for themselves. New players tend to avoid this even though it's rather obvious. It can make a world of difference in your gameplay.

With that, we've covered some of the most important things to cover in this chapter. We've successfully worked through the nine biggest mistakes that new players constantly make. In the chapters to follow, we're going to build on this knowledge in order to help you become the best player possible in no time.

Chapter 2: Advanced Tips

So, let's cut to the chase: you want real information about how you can become an excellent Fortnite player in no time. You want things that will take you from zero to hero in Fortnite. That's understandable and even noble. This chapter is filled with tips that are designed to turn your gameplay all the way up.

Tip #1: Always Keep Moving

The first advanced tip is actually pretty simple. No matter what, be moving around. Fortnite is a game of activity, and it's extremely fast paced to boot. No matter what, make it as difficult as possible for people to aim at you and end up killing you.

If you keep moving around then you make it really difficult for people to figure out what it is that you're going to do. This is the first key to surviving through the rough early and middle parts of a round of Fortnite. If you leave yourself open, then you're going to just expose yourself to a lot of danger. Make yourself hard to hit and it will pay off by keeping you alive for longer.

Tip #2: Play Mind Games by Closing Doors

This tip is an easy one to miss, but it can have a huge impact with next to no effort on your end. Use closed or open doors in order to manipulate your enemies into doing what you want them to. If you close doors behind you when you enter a building, you can make it look like nobody's been in there. Then you can wait out enemies from the inside and take them out when they come around.

You can also choose to leave doors open and then use that as a means of intimidating enemies by letting them know that there's danger afoot. This can throw them off, especially if you couple it with not being where they expect you to be should they decide to enter.

Tip #3: Always Pick Up Ammo

Ammo is absolutely indispensable in Fortnite. You

do not want to be running out of ammo, so you need to be doing what you can to ensure that you're getting ammo crates no matter what. It doesn't take long to open and loot an ammo crate, and if you do, you can also ensure that nobody else benefits from the ammo crate that you left unopened. Remember to always get these, because you know for sure that ammo is better than not having it, so you have no reason not to.

Tip #4: Dual Wielding

A fact that a lot of people don't think about is the fact that you can equip two of the same exact weapon. If you do this, you never have to worry about reload time. You can fire off one round and then switch to the other equipped version of that same weapon. This makes firing rounds a seamless activity and gives you an easy advantage in duels. Depending upon your playstyle, if you tend to play more aggressively then this could be a great option. Once you get used to playing in this fashion, you can use this in order to pull off some really powerful moves on people. Picking up speed with this is the key to really excelling with it!

With these four simple tips, you'll already be on the path to putting yourself far above the other players that you'll be facing. The thing you have to realize is that a lot of people who play Fortnite do so casually, so by even taking an interest into how you can improve your play and be above them, you're putting yourself ahead. If you are to go a step further and start implementing all of these things into your play, you put yourself in a position such that you can easily and quickly become one of the best in many of your matches.

Chapter 3: Best In-Game Strategies to Go from Noob to Pro Quickly

In this chapter, we're going to be discussing the best strategies to go from somebody who is relatively unfamiliar with Fortnite or even Battle Royale games in general to somebody who feels confident playing the game in a way that makes you a master.

One of the most important things to do in this realm is to adopt what is called the *metagame*. Therefore, this chapter is going to be based around the strategies you can use in order to build your concept of the *metagame*.

What is a metagame? A metagame is known as the *game within a game*. It's the game which goes beyond the simple mechanics of the game into those things which actually outline the strategy within the game itself.

For example, let's say there's a game with 30

different people you can play and 10 different weapons they can use, regardless of the actual way the game is played. The metagame withdraws somewhat from the mechanics of the game itself and the idea of just what the game *is* to what the best way to *play* the game is.

Therefore, the metagame would be based around the idea of the way that the game is *played*, how best to *win* the game, what the best *characters and weapons* are, and so on and so forth. Discussing metagame means discussing those concepts which require thought rather than sheer mechanical skill.

Every game has a metagame when it becomes competitive, because the competitive aspect of a game completely revolves around the game's metagame. Even chess and poker have metagames - it's not just reserved for complicated virtual games.

So without further ado, let's start thinking about things in ways that will help you improve your knowledge of in-game strategies and your knowledge of the game *within* the game of Fortnite.

Tip #1: Understanding the Concept of Resources

Resources are important in any game, and every game can be seen as a game of draining your opponent's resources until you win. The exact way that this happens doesn't particularly matter too much for the discussion just involving the idea of resources.

What could be considered a resource in Fortnite? Well, pretty much anything that determines whether you win and whether your opponent loses. Resources are anything that gives a player an advantage.

Weapons, therefore, could be considered a resource. The actual *resources* in Fortnite like wood, brick, and metal could be seen as resources. However, it goes deeper than this. Your opponent's *health* and *ammo* are also resources.

Winning games is about getting an advantage and then building on that advantage until you win. You gain an advantage partly by depleting your opponent of their resources. If you can keep chipping away at their resources, then you can start winning pretty easily. Always be thinking about how you can get *more* resources for yourself and ensure *less* resources for everybody else. This doesn't even have to be on an individual level. For example, if you were to *take* an ammo crate, even if you don't need it really, you still ensure that nobody else can *get* the ammo crate.

Tip #2: Plan Your Game from the Start

Professional players understand the importance of planning their games from the very beginning. Regardless of the game, every player in every major competitive game has some sort of plan from the very beginning. For example, in League of Legends, junglers will often have their route planned from the very beginning and will just modify it in relation to how the game is going. In Dota, the beginning of a game is often highly choreographed by the team, and the nature and meta of the game itself demand that they move in high synchronicity with one another.

For this reason, having a solid idea of the course of the game, how it plays out, and what you can do over said course will allow you to better plan your game altogether and have a better idea of what to do when.

For this, you need to think about the game. How does the game go in sequence? First, players drop. Then, players gather resources. Eventually, the circle closes. People pick each other off until there's only two left. Last man standing wins. End game. Easy, right?

There's a lot that happens within that that makes it harder, though. Planning around these things can allow you to become a better player. For example, if you know that the storm is going to come eventually and your fort on the edge of the map is going to be worthless, is it worth building the fort in the first place since the materials are just going to be wasted?

Additionally, a lot of higher-skill Fortnite players will develop what's called a route. The purpose of a route is to give the player something to do at the start of the game in terms of gathering loot and ammo while avoiding death as much as possible and procuring the best items possible. You'll develop your own route with time based on the state of the game and the things you find most effective for you.

Even the idea of a route, however, has a lot to do with the idea of planning your game out. So think about that: how do you want your game to play out, and when you think realistically about how Fortnite games *play* out, what can you do to reasonably ensure that plan will happen?

Tip #3: Don't Underestimate Mind games

In the last chapter, one of the tips was to use doors in order to play tricks on your opponents. What we failed to do at that point, though, was go into greater detail on how that idea of mind games can be used in order to make you a better player overall.

All people are fallible, and all people make mistakes. Realizing this is crucial to realizing that you can win any game you're in, it's just about knowing what to do when and making less mistakes than your opponents. Even the best players in the world of any given game will make mistakes; the difference between them and worse players is just that they make fewer.

The perfect example of mind games rests in poker. There's even an extremely popular phrase, "poker face", which refers to the ability to not give away information through your expressions, which is much easier said than done. There is also value in able to being able to *bluff* in poker, as well as to be able to *call bluffs* and to see through your opponent's deceptions, information, and intimidation.

Mind games apply a lot to Fortnite as well. People

can still be intimidated in virtual games, especially when they're games that get you as invested as Fortnite does. Being able to get inside your opponent's head and meaningfully predict what they're going to do is an important component of playing against other people.

The best way to start understanding mind games is firstly to start being mindful yourself. Instead of allowing yourself to get caught up in your emotions in the game, try to be as stoic, detached, and reasonable as possible in your assessment of the game.

However, that's only the start of the battle. It's also important that you start to consider what you would be doing in your enemy's situation. This is a really high level of processing, and when you're trying to juggle all of the game's mechanics at once, it can be pretty difficult to really get to this level. However, once you *do* get to this level, things will be much easier. Always be thinking about what you would do if you were your enemy.

This actually serves to benefit you in two ways. If your enemy is equally skilled or worse than you, it will cause you to often win trades and duels because you'll be one step ahead of them. However, if your enemy is *better* than you and you pay attention to what they do, and what they do *deviates* from what you would have done and they end up winning the duel, then you can actually learn from what they did. The most important thing is that you're constantly learning to observe people who are better than you and incorporate the things that they do into your gameplay.

This ties in really well to the fourth tip as well:

Tip #4: Learn Humility and Grace

This seems almost cliché, but it's the simple truth about sports psychology, and playing games at a high level most definitely falls under the umbrella of sports psychology. If you want to become a better player, then you need to learn to start playing your games with both humility and grace. Let's tackle these concepts one at a time.

What I mean by humility is that you need to accept that no matter how good you get, you are never the best. Even if you were to become the best, if you start to slack off or play overconfidently, your chances of losing skyrocket because you start to get cocky. Playing in a cocky way is no way to win, and you can't expect to start winning if you're playing cockily. If you play cockily, you start to underthink your moves and your opponent's moves and just assume that you know best. This is especially crucial to overcome when you *aren't* good at the game yet, because doing so when you aren't quite good at the game yet can lead to you never having the ability to truly develop. Realize that you are bad, and that you'll be bad for quite a while. That's the best way to get better.

The other way to get better is through learning grace, by which I mean learning to not get excessively angry in the face of loss. In games that are as competitive and stressful as Fortnite, it can be a major stress reaction to start getting angry. However, this actually keeps you from growing as a player at all because it reduces your ability to really process fairly and honestly everything that's happening. More than that, you tend to become prone to *tilt*.

What is *tilt*? Tilt is the term in the gaming community for when your gameplay gets worse due to frustration while playing a game that keeps adding up and adding up. When you go on tilt or become tilted, your entire gameplay starts to slip up, eventually leading to you just needing to take a break from the game. What's the best way to avoid going on tilt, then? The best way is to avoid becoming so frustrated with the game in the first place, and the best way to do *that* is by letting yourself process everything that happens without anger at all.

Really, the best way to get good at a game and become a master of the metagame is to control your emotions and use them to your advantage. Stay calm, cool, and collected. Doing so, you're in the best mindframe to really improve at the game. Just following these simple tips will allow you to become better than most of the players out there.

With that, we've cracked open the metagame and explored many of the concepts pertaining to it. It's through mastery of the metagame and the game mechanics themselves that you're going to really propel yourself forward, but raw game mechanics will only get you so far. Because of this, at some point in your journey, it will be necessary that you start to hone your knowledge of the metagame and the more complex parts of Fortnite at the competitive level.

Chapter 4: The Big Difference Between PUBG and Fortnite - Building Structures

Fortnite, believe it or not, was not the first major battle royale game. Before Fortnite was PUBG, and before PUBG was a game called H1Z1. PUBG, however, was the first to catch a lot of traction when streamers started picking up the game and playing it.

If you're coming from PUBG to Fortnite, it can be as stark of a contrast as moving from a game like Dota to League of Legends or from Starcraft to Age of Empires; while the games and mechanics are rather similar, there will be some essential changes in gameplay that can make a world of difference in terms of gameplay and how the overall rhythm of the game plays out.

One of the major differences in mechanics between PUBG and Fortnite is that Fortnite introduced something that PUBG didn't: the idea of building structures. In this chapter, we're going to try to discuss the idea of building structures at a depth appropriate to bring you up to speed if you happened to come from PUBG.

So what is building? It's self-explanatory, really. In Fortnite, you pick up resources over the course of the match, and you can then use these in order to build structures in order to protect yourself. You can also use these structures strategically in one way or another.

This small mechanical addition makes a massive difference in the way that the game plays out overall. For example, the introduction of structural building means that the end of a game of Fortnite usually comes down to two players trying to outmaneuver each other in terms of their building.

From the start of every Fortnite game, you should be gathering resources that you can later use in order to build structures. If you don't do so, then you're setting yourself up for failure later on. Resources are such a fundamental part of Fortnite that you can't skip this step.

One general tip for newer Fortnite players is that there shouldn't be a point at which you aren't gathering resources. If you're moving from one point to another or just trying to move around the map, you should be stopping to get resources whenever possible.

Do not, however, make yourself a sitting duck. Gathering resources takes a second, and you leave yourself open - if only briefly - to the aggression of other players. This is not an enviable position to be in, and it could wind up with you dead - *not* what you want to happen.

However, once you do have materials, you can start using them in order to defend yourself. For example, you can build what's called a *panic fort* as we'll talk about later on in the book, or any other number of things designed to protect you in extremely stressful situations.

For now, that's a cursory introduction to the concept of building, which is something which really divides Fortnite from other games in its class and sets it apart from its competitors, as well as provides one of the highest skill ceilings for people who are new to the game and coming from another one.

Chapter 5: How Weapons Work

In this chapter, we're going to be covering a bunch of things to help you gain a better understanding of the exact ways that weapons work in Fortnite. The system can be pretty intricate if you're unfamiliar with it, but it will definitely become more familiar to you as you work with it more.

The first thing we need to cover is the way that weapons are divided. Weapons are broken up by a rarity system. These rarities describe both how common the weapon is as well as how good of a quality it is. The weapon rarity system can be divided into five categories: *common, uncommon, rare, epic,* and *legendary.*

Common weapons are coded with *gray.* These have the base stats of any given weapon.

Uncommon weapons are coded with *green.* These are slightly better than *common* weapons.

Rare weapons are coded with blue, and these are

when you start to get into particularly good stats. Rare weapons are worth seeking out, and will put you above the competition.

Epic weapons are purple, and are the second best tier. These weapons have particularly strong stats and if you happen to loot one, you are fortunate.

Legendary weapons are the best tier available for weaponry, and have the best stats of all the tiers consequentially. You should be seeking out legendary weapons whenever possible and trying to do everything in your power to get ahold of them.

Weapons of the same type can have different rarities. In these cases, rarities describe just the scaling stats of the weapon as well as how rare it is to find that weapon with those specific stats. So, for example, a burst-fire assault rifle of uncommon rarity will have better stats than a burst-fire assault rifle of common rarity.

Items, for the record, work in much the same way.

Everything in Fortnite is coded according to rarity, which can help you to determine how beneficial they are to you and how much they can do for you.

The next thing we need to talk about is the actual *qualities* of the weapons in Fortnite, such as how they feel when you shoot them.

First and foremost, weapons in Fortnite have *recoil*. This can impact how your aim shifts around after a shot, and it's hard to account for if you're shooting multiple bullets in a row. This is something that you're going to need to get used to depending upon the fighting games that you're coming from.

Aside from that, weapons follow *hitscan*. This means that as soon as you shoot a bullet at an enemy, their health drops in accordance to where you hit them. This means, in other words, that Fortnite doesn't account for things like bullet drop. This stands in contrast to games like PUBG, where bullet drop plays a pretty major factor in how your shots play out and all weapons experience bullet drop. In Fortnite, the only places that you can expect bullet drop to occur are when you're shooting sniper rifles. Bullet drop happens in no other instance.

When you shoot a bullet, a tracer will follow it. This is important in a tactical sense, because it can alert enemies to your location when you shoot at them. However, you can also use this to your advantage. If someone shoots near you, you can follow the tracer to figure out exactly where they're shooting from. This can easily shift a duel in your advantage if they mess up their initial shot.

Another thing you need to be aware about is the fact that, well, guns are noisy. In fact, one of the quickest ways to give away your position in Fortnite is to shoot. Things are louder in Fortnite than they are in other games, and your shots can and will give you away. You need to be wary of this before you ever shoot a bullet.

However, this shouldn't be allowed to deter you from aggressive play. Camping doesn't necessarily win in Fortnite, and a lot of the time, aggression is rewarded. Don't be afraid to play aggressively, just be aware of the noise that you're making in the process.

Chapter 6: How to Use the Storm to Your Advantage

One way that Fortnite differs from PUBG is that Fortnite massively discourages camping. While in PUBG, camping is massively rewarded both by the size of the map as well as by the game mechanics itself, in Fortnite, it's shut down entirely by mechanics within the game as well as by the general pace of the game itself.

One of the major ways that Fortnite tries to discourage camping is through what's called *the storm*. As the game progresses, eventually the usable size of the map will shrink. This happens through the development of a large circle called the *storm*. The storm starts at the outer edges of the map and over the course of the game will shrink down into a much smaller area to contain the smaller number of players as the game presses on.

If you're caught outside the storm, you start to lose health. This means that if you were to just stay outside of the storm once the storm eventually shrinks, you would end up dying.

However, you don't die instantly by any means. The health tax by the storm is actually pretty low and pretty slow, which means that you can use the storm to your tactical advantage both by being inside of it and outside of it. In this chapter, we're going to cover a few different ways that you can do so in order to improve your play and start winning more matches.

Strategy #1: Keep Your Back to the Storm

This is one of the most basic ways to use the storm to your advantage. When the storm is shrinking, most people will be decking it to get inside, especially at lower levels of play. You can take advantage of this by keeping pace with the storm on the rim of it. Doing such will give you the ability to pick people off as the storm closes in, while keeping you safe from the people who are trying to do the same thing. Do try to remain somewhat aware of your surroundings though, as there is the chance that someone may be behind you within the

storm and could get a kill in you. As always, you
need to keep moving no matter what and avoid
making yourself an easy target.

With that said, if you can stay on the edge of the
storm, you can pretty easily find a way to pick
people off as it closes in.

Strategy #2: Keep Your Eyes to the Storm

Alternatively, once you have an idea of the rate at
which the storm closes in, you can get ahead of the
curve when the storm starts to close in a bit more
by heading inward before other people do. This will
allow you to start to pick people off as they come *in*
with the storm. There will be a lot of people trying
to beat the storm and by giving yourself time to get
ahead of them and set up a bit more in a more
central area, you allow yourself the opportunity to
pick them off while they're just trying to get to
safety.

Chapter 7: The 5 Best Weapons

In Fortnite, there are a huge number of different guns that you can use. All of these guns have their own strengths and weaknesses, and they all have different feels. For this reason, it's difficult to just break down five different weapons that you should consider the best. With that said, you *do* have five inventory slots, so it only makes sense to tell you the five weapons that I find to be the absolute best in the game.

There's a chance that this may not be the list of the five best weapons for *you* specifically, because everybody has their own natural strengths and what works for most people may in fact not work for you. So do play around and try to find the things that you find to be the absolute best for yourself.

#1: The SCAR Assault Rifle

This weapon is one of the best in the game, hands

down, at least as of the time of writing. However, it's a pretty rare drop so you're going to have to get one either through loot chests or through playing more aggressively and getting kills on people that you think may have them.

That said, if you do manage to get your hands on one, you'll be amazed by how consistently great it is. For example, it's very accurate, it does a lot of damage, and it's equally useful regardless of how close to the enemy you are. If you can get ahold of this and play smart, there's no reason that you shouldn't win whatever game you find it in.

#2: The Rocket Launcher

The rocket launcher is extremely versatile in Fortnite. It serves its purpose pretty fantastically by allowing you to both destroy enemy structures with ease or to decimate a group of enemies that you see standing together.

However, it does have its particular advantages; while you can use it to rack up kills, this isn't the best way to use it. It's best at destroying structures or natural elements. This makes it, however, an excellent offensive part of your arsenal since you can just destroy enemy forts and then aggress them with another weapon. Be sure to pick it up if you get the opportunity, because you'll dominate the game afterward.

#3: Pump Shotgun

Many people will say that the tactical shotgun is better than the pump shotgun. Others still will say that the heavy shotgun is better than either. However, I'm of the camp that say that the pump shotgun is the best option of the three.

The simple fact is that while the pump shotgun has the lowest fire rate of the three, it packs the most damage. For the situations where you're going to be using a shotgun, damage is the thing that matters above all else. Fire rate can take a back seat to damage. Not to mention the crazy amount of damage that higher-end pump shotguns can do - it's going to be hard to find something that can match up.

For the kind of close-range or closed-environment situations that you would actually use a shotgun in, there simply isn't a match for the pump shotgun. Prioritize having one of these in your inventory, because you're going to need a weapon for close-range anyway.

#4: Bolt-Action Sniper

At some point, you're going to need to kill somebody at a distance. When that time comes, you'd be at a loss if you weren't properly equipped for it. There's no weapon to better equip you for this than the bolt-action sniper rifle.

This gun has an incredible over 200 damage for every headshot, and still an amazing amount of power for anything that isn't a headshot. There's nothing better for killing an enemy at a long-distance than this gun, which makes it an essential especially in the mid-game where you're trying to strategically set up for the storm and then pick people off.

#5: Suppressed Pistol

This gun used to not be as popular, but it is definitely coming around. The reason is that it does almost as much damage as assault rifles for every shot, and the only limitation is how fast you can fire it.

Essentially, this means that while it's not as good as the SCAR, it does stand alongside the burst-fire assault rifle and the M16 assault rifle. This one, however, has an added bonus. Even though the fire rate can be as much, if not more, than the burst-fire assault rifle depending on how fast you can fire, you also receive the added perk that the gun is silenced. This means it doesn't make nearly as much noise as the AR or the burst-rifle. This is especially important when you're either within earshot of one and only one enemy, or you otherwise would just like to keep your location as under wraps as possible.

In a game like Fortnite where noise makes a huge amount of difference, there's nothing quite as important as being sure that you limit the amount of noise that you make. If you can do that, then your chances of surviving through the game shoot up.

With that, we've worked through the five best weapons in Fortnite, in my opinion. The thing that really makes a difference with all of these, though, is how much you practice with them and how good you get with them. Having, for example, a SCAR doesn't matter at all if you yourself can't hit anything.

Chapter 8: Map Showing Best Chest Locations

This chapter is self-explanatory. I've prepared a map with the locations of chests all over the map, and circled some of the best places for you to go in order to secure some great loot quickly and safely.

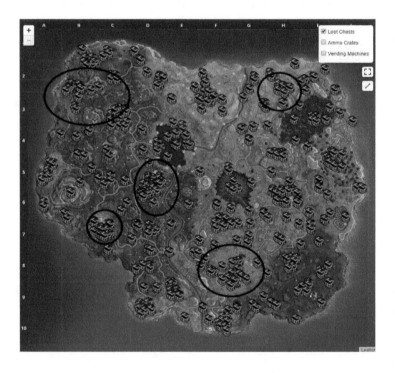

Chapter 9: Mastering Panic Forts

In Fortnite, there are few things more fundamental than having a good idea of how to build panic forts in a pinch. Panic forts offer you a fool-proof way to defend yourself when push comes to shove.

Remember how earlier in the book we talked about how better players, when they're in trouble, will spare no timing starting to construct things in order to defend themselves. One of the most important of these structures is the panic fort.

Panic forts go by many other names, but what they generally refer to is a fort that is one wall wide by one wall long. Panic forts provide the perfect combination of cover and vantage, and they also allow you to build up with ease should you decide that you need a greater height advantage.

Being able to build a panic fort in a jiffy is an extremely important exercise to master within Fortnite. There's a lot more to it than you may think, too. We're going to start with a really basic definition of what a panic fort is and how you can use it in order to gain a specific advantage in Fortnite.

So what is a panic fort? It's a small fort that you can build in a crunch in order to ensure that enemies both don't have a direct line of sight at you while also ensuring that you can look out and scope the area out. You can build them in a crunch when getting shot at or in a vulnerable position in order to allow yourself to safely return fire against other players.

How do you build a basic panic fort? Well, what you do is firstly make sure that you're using wood. Wood is a lot harder to break than brick or metal when you first put it down, and there's also just a lot more of it available than there is of brick or metal. As such, it's the perfect choice for any sort of temporary protection structure.

Build four basic wood walls around you. If you're building it in response to somebody shooting at you, then you place the wall in front of you first and go from there. From here, you now want to jump and place a ramp below yourself. You can scoot downward on the ramp in order to take cover, then move forward on the ramp in order to have height advantage.

You don't want to build this in response to somebody; rather, you want to use it when you feel that somebody is coming or that somebody may be shooting at you soon. This sets the duel up in a very advantageous way and allows you to have a height advantage on the enemy. It also allows you an opportunity to build up from wherever you are. You can keep building this over and over, too. For example, you can jump up and place a floor, then build another level to the panic fort.

You can build onto this by actually building a larger structures. If you build a rectangle instead of a 1x1 square, then you can place a ramp leading up either side and then have build where you can escape to the center and then peek out either side.

Lastly, you can build what you can call the *funnel*. To do this, you build a two wall by two wall box, then you stand in the center of this and place a ramp leading into the center on each side, so it starts to look like it's sucking you in. From here, you can also build outwards with floors and walls in order to build yourself a really strong but simple fort with a lot of cover.

You can combine these with things like editing structures and builds in order to make them even stronger or more sophisticated. There is quite a lot to how you can edit different structures after you place them, but the possibilities are virtually endless and you can build a really fantastic fort in no time.

The real perk of panic forts is that while they aren't terribly nuanced bases, they do give you a really great position whether you're in a duel, preparing for one, or preparing for an all-out firefight. They scale well whether you're playing in groups or solo/duo, and they break down easily when you're done with them, should you want to break them back down.

The best way to practice them is by playing and using them. You're only going to get good at them if you actually try to implement them into your play, and in order to do that you need to actually *play*. It should go without saying that the only way to get good at Fortnite is to play it, so you need to do that!

Chapter 10: Best 4 New Landing Spots

In earlier chapters, we talked about the massive importance of starting out strong in Fortnite, and we also talked about how eventually you'd start to build up a sort of route for each round that you can follow in order to get the results you're after. The most important part of any Fortnite game is the start, where everything in the game world is up for grabs as well as when you're most vulnerable in general.

In order to deal with this situation and help you know the best places to land in order to start the game out strong, I've compiled a lot of the four best landing spots in Fortnite.

Spot #1: Near Tilted Towers

Tilted Towers is often considered to be one of the best places for newcomers to drop anyway, because it's one of the lowest difficulty regions in the game. Because of this, it can be alluring to drop off at the

Tilted Towers, especially as a new player.

When you drop near the Tilted Towers, a little bit to the left of them you'll see a large pool near a bunch of land. When you drop here, you'll find a lot of stuff to stock up on. Land here in order to stock up and then start heading to Tilted Towers. From there, you can start thinning the herd.

Spot #2: Snobby Shores

This is one of the first places that the bus will fly over, so if you can actually make it here then there won't be many people to give you trouble just yet. Around Snobby Shores, there are a lot of different houses that are full of things that will let you gear up. Be sure to look in the basement of each home as well, because that's where you're going to find a lot more useful gear.

Spot #3: The Moisty Mire

This place is often understated. Nobody really goes here, since it's covered in water. This means that people who go here are slowed down when they pass through it. By extension, you aren't going to run into a lot of people. There are several crates here and a whole lot of resources that are absolutely free for you to take.

The only thing you need to be careful about here is planning your getaway, because the terrain of the area is not incredibly friendly. However, barring that, this is an excellent place to start out the match.

Spot #4: Near Anarchy Acres

Right around Anarchy Acres, there's a motel. If you land on top of this motel and then break in, you'll find that there is a huge amount of loot that will let you get off to a fantastic start. You'll come out way ahead. It's also pretty secluded and there aren't really going to be many people out here. This means that there's a ton of loot, even though the location is pretty safe. This is actually one of the best landing spots in the whole game. Be sure to take advantage of its incredible opportunity.

With that, we've covered the four most impressive landing spots in the game. For your reference, I've included a map to help you find the locations when you're dropping down from above, along with crate locations. Good luck!

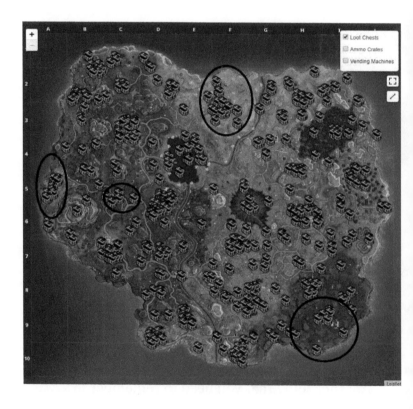

Chapter 11: Building Tips

In this chapter, we're going to be going over some of the best tips for building effectively. We've already talked a bit about things like building panic forts, but we haven't talked about the process of building itself.

The first thing that you need to bear in mind is something that we've likely already talked about in passing, but it's something we need to mention right now and really try to drive home: try your best to be harvesting whenever you can. If you're moving around the map, make sure that you're always getting materials. This goes beyond the metagame principle of just taking materials from somebody else who could have them and bleeds into the fact that the more materials you have, the more leniency that you have in building.

Another thing that you need to remember in building is that building is not easy, nor is it quiet. When you're building, you cause a lot of ruckus that can really easily alert enemies to your position and put you in a vulnerable spot. Remember when you build that you are not putting yourself in a favorable position.

In terms of general gameplay, you should be prioritizing wood as your main building material. Although more complex materials do become important as the game goes on, they take a longer time to build. Wood has a relatively high health immediately upon being placed, but it doesn't go up much from there. By contrast, brick and metal both have low starting healths but become much stronger as they're being built.

Wood also takes the least time to build and is more abundant than anything else. Make sure that you're getting wood before anything else, as you're going to be using wood quite often when you're playing. There are not many circumstances aside from your final base where you ought to prefer wood over anything else.

Also, you don't need to waste your resources with complex forts early on. The map always shrinks a ton as the game goes on, which makes any early forts you build outside the storm pretty much worthless. Instead, you need to be saving your resources for the full fort that you're going to be building at the end of the game.

In essence, don't waste your time and energy and put yourself in a vulnerable position by spending too much time building before you really need to. This just leads to you having a harder time as the game drags on and potentially leads to you running out of resources later - that is, if you survive after giving your position away early.

Don't just think about the things you can build in terms of forts and structures. They have a lot of uses beyond just that. For example, you can pretty easily use ramps in order to reach places where you wouldn't be able to reach otherwise and gain a height advantage that way. You can build platforms really easily in order to get around the map, and then later use that platform as an element of your fort if you so desire.

It's also important that you know that you can edit structures. Editing structures in Fortnite after you've placed them is really important and can lead to some really diverse and complex structures, and also give you the opportunity to make a counterplay where you wouldn't otherwise be able to.

For example, you can edit the blueprint of a wall in order to add a window. This window can give you a little safe vantage point from which you can peek out and shoot at the enemy. You can also edit a door into the wall behind you in a panic fort for a sneaky getaway. The options are endless, and learning how to edit structures can really open up the possible gameplay mechanics.

Chapter 12: Fun Fortnite Challenges

A lot of the fun of Fortnite comes from the things that you can do outside of the context of the game itself. For example, while the game does set you up with an extremely fun game mode from the very start, you can do challenges within that game mode to make it even more fun for yourself.

This chapter is based around documenting a lot of different challenges that you can try to do in order to give the game a new dimension for yourself. Give some of these a try and see if you enjoy them!

The first challenge you should try out is the *always moving challenge*. In this challenge, you try to challenge yourself to constantly be moving, even if you're aiming. This builds on the thing we outlined in the advanced tips chapter about always remaining in motion. It's a very fun challenge that really puts your ability to play to the test and keeps you on your toes.

The second challenge you should try is the *hardmode challenge*. This challenge is just a normal round of Fortnite, but with one small change: you aren't allowed to use any shields or healing. In essence, any damage that you take over the course of the game is permanent damage and you aren't allowed to heal or shield any of it. This one is really hard and tests your ability to survive and avoid enemies. It can be great for building those skills!

The third challenge you should try is the *no building challenge*. In this challenge, you simply go the whole game avoiding building at all costs. You cannot build panic forts nor any sort of protection for yourself, and you can't use building in order to traverse the map at all. You're just stuck with what you can do on your own accord.

The fourth challenge is *common weapons only*. Give this challenge a go by refusing to use any weapons that aren't common. This puts you against players who may or may not be better than you but who do, for certain, have better stats than you do.

It's a real test of skill and isn't for the faint of heart.

In a similar vein, you may want to try out the *pistol only challenge*. This challenge, too, isn't for the faint of heart; you're just holding yourself off with a pistol against everybody else on the map. No other weapons at all, though you can build at your leisure.

You can also try to kill people with only grenades. You aren't allowed to get kills on anybody using anything that isn't a grenade. This one can be especially difficult because grenades aren't super common so you have to be really careful about how you manage your ammunition.

Also try the solo squads challenge. In the solo squad challenge, what you do is go into squad mode then turn on *no fill*. In essence, you're the only solo player going up against a bunch of people on squads. Your chances of winning aren't super high, but that's the fun of the challenge. Try your best to hold off the others around you and end up with a victory royale!

More than that, you can try the *only one challenge.* In this challenge, you only allow yourself to loot one house. If you don't come upon much in that house, then tough luck. This challenge is extremely difficult. However, you can make it easier by allowing yourself to loot enemies after you kill them, if you'd like.

Those are just a few of the different challenges that you can do in Fortnite in order to challenge yourself and present a harder gameplay experience than usual. The cool thing about doing challenges in Fortnite is that since the game is every man for themselves, you aren't disadvantaging somebody by doing challenges as you would in Dota or another team-based game. This means you can go your own pace and, in the end, do whatever you like. Enjoy!

Conclusion

With that, we've made it through to the end of *Fortnite Battle Royale*. Fortnite is a hard game with a lot of concepts that you have to learn to start being better at it. It can be extremely frustrating to deal with being bad at a game, and the simple fact is that nobody likes to be bad at a game.

The next step is to start doing all of this to improve yourself. Take advantage of this knowledge in order to grow as a player. This isn't going to happen overnight. In fact, you're probably going to find that it's extremely frustrating a lot of the time, and that's okay. It's okay to be frustrated with competitive games. Nobody likes the process of improving, everybody just wants to be the best right away.

Do remember, though. It's not a sprint, it's a marathon. You can become a great Fortnite player really quickly in no time flat by implementing the tracks in this book. You can also build on that knowledge in order to become a better player over time, and that's more realistically how it's all going to work out. Using the skills in this book, you'll become good rather quickly, but then what? At one point or another, unfortunately, you're going to plateau, and it's at these points that you're going to experience the most frustration in terms of your overall play. However, if you can just bite the bullet and keep going forward with it, then you can always get through these plateaus and become a better player. Fortunately, the things that we covered in the metagame part of this book will help you to achieve that as well.

I wish you the best of luck in your endeavour. Finally, if you found this book useful in anyway, a review on Amazon is always appreciated!